SPOTTING
FOR
NELLIE

Pamela Lowell

MARSHALL CAVENDISH

Marshall Cavendish Corporation
99 White Plains Road
Tarrytown, NY 10591
www.marshallcavendish.us/kids

The line on page 41 is from "Trenchtown"
by Bob Marley and the Wailers: *Trenchtown Rock* © 2002, Trojan Records.

The lines on pages 48, 139, 190, and 289 are from *Make the Team: Gymnastics for Girls: A Gold Medal Guide for Great Gymnastics* by Steve Whitlock for the U.S. Gymnastics Federation © 1991, Little, Brown.

The lines on pages 62 and 150 are from *Making a Living Alongshore: Digging Clams* © 1978 motherearthnews.com.

The lines on pages 67, 160, and 208 are from: Carpenter, *Gymnastics for Girls and Women*, © 1985, Parker Publishing Company, Inc. Reproduced by permission of Pearson Education, Inc.

The line on page 72 is from "The Adventures of Jimmy Neutron: Boy Genius" by Thumb Wars © 2002, Nickelodeon.

The lines on page 83 are from the song "Hallelujah." Lyrics © 1988 by Leonard Cohen and Sony/ATV Music Publishing Canada company.

The lines on page 88 are from *Quahog*, "Rhode Island Sea Grant Fact Sheet" by Eleanor Ely © 1998.

The line on page 96 is from *Listening in the Silence, Seeing in the Dark* by Ruthann Knechel Johansen © 2002, University of California Press.

The lines on page 133 are from the *Star Trek* TV series. "The Menagerie" by Gene Roddenberry © 1966.

The line on page 154 is from the article "Presenting a United Front" by Alex Kuffner © 2007, *Providence Journal*.

The line on page 172 is from "Song #40" by Dave Matthews Band. Lyrics © Colden Grey, Ltd.

The lines on page 178 are from *The Complete Poems of Emily Dickinson*, edited by Thomas H. Johnson, and are in the public domain.

The lines on page 274 are from *Secrets of Shellfishing* by Edward Ricciuti © 1982, Big Country Books (Hancock House Publishers).

The lines on page 281 are excerpted from Mrs. Robinson's blog © 2007. www.carteretcountyschools.org, Jessica Robinson.

Library of Congress Cataloging-in-Publication Data
Lowell, Pamela.
Spotting for Nellie / by Pamela Lowell. — 1st ed.
p. cm.
Summary: After a terrible car accident leaves her sister brain-injured, sixteen-year-old Claire struggles with guilt for the accident, helping her sister recover, and boyfriend problems.
Includes bibliographical references.
ISBN 978-0-7614-5583-7
[1. Brain—Wounds and injuries—Fiction. 2. Sisters—Fiction. 3. Family life—Rhode Island—Fiction. 4. Rhode Island—Fiction.] I. Title.
PZ7.L9646Sp 2009
[Fic]—dc22
2008053619

Book design by Becky Terhune
Editor: Marilyn Brigham

Printed in China (E)
First edition

10 9 8 7 6 5 4 3 2 1

Marshall Cavendish

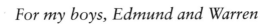

For my boys, Edmund and Warren

PROLOGUE

There is only one girl left in the gym. She's wearing her practice leotard. Her left knee is braced, and chalk dusts her feet. It's late, which is part of the reason she just fell.

It hurt—but she doesn't expect any sympathy, not from the man in sweatpants and sneakers who is watching her closely. "You okay?" he says, more of a statement than a question. He's pacing back and forth on the wooden floor, as if he's at the end of an invisible chain.

The blue mats she has landed on are tired looking, like the gymnast. She's been here since early afternoon, and now it's nearly ten. She just missed an easy release move on the uneven bars. And she hasn't done that in years!

Splat, she went down, flat on her stomach—a dead fish.

Or a *poisson mort*. Which reminds her, she still has homework to do. In French class they're studying sea terms: *au bord de la mer*. And in biology, classifications. A test tomorrow in each.

"Enough for tonight?" She walks over to her gym bag. But before she glances back, she knows that (as usual) it's not enough.

"Was that even *you* just now?" he replies. "Think about it. That's going to be your last?"

She knows exactly what he's talking about but doesn't answer.

"What's with the face? We've been through this before." His voice grows impatient. "You have to *want* to be the best."

"I *do*, Dad."

And the gymnast does. She thinks she does, anyway. But lately it's been confusing. Especially when every landing, every dismount, makes her knee feel like it's been punctured by a shard of broken glass.

She ripped a meniscus last fall. It's taken a long time to come back from this injury. X-rays. Surgery. Almost four months of physical therapy. She sat on the sidelines day after day, when all she really wanted to do was fly across those dusty mats; or stick a perfect landing; to shimmer, to hover, to soar.

But now that she can, she's not sure *what* she wants.

Coach says she has great lines; poise, maturity, a drive for perfection. The judges seem to think so, too. And her father, well, he says she's destined for gold. But he never mentions that in front of her sister. And now her parents are talking about shipping her off to Texas next fall, to train.

Think about it; you'll be with the best in the world. Isn't that exciting? We'll find the money somehow, if that's what you want.

Right now all she wants is to go home.

The last mistake you make is the one you'll sleep with tonight. That's what her father always says. Fine. She'll do it again. One more time.

The gymnast grasps the low bar and swings her legs, up and over, gathering momentum. Pausing, arms strong, she transitions onto the high bar, extending her legs to a perfect handstand. Pirouette. Then hand over hand, release, grab, pike. She has a natural, fluid swing. Transition, salto, release.

This is what she does. Day after day after day. Just like a job.

Not like a job, she realizes; most people get to go home after eight hours.

Circling now, like the second hand on a clock (but much faster), she sweeps around the high bar, defying gravity: the giants, her favorite. Then finally her dismount, a double twist with a tuck. And despite her braced left knee, she sticks it. Not even a step. Before she looks at her father, she swallows the pain.

"Better," he says. "Don't forget to smile. You want them to think it's easy. Like you're having fun, right?"

"Right, Dad." She shrugs and picks up her bag.

There is a secret she keeps close to her. She hasn't told anyone yet. Not her coach. Not her sister—or her other teammates. And especially not her father.

A part of her remembers a time *before*. When everything wasn't riding on her success—or failure. When fun was easy, like doing crazy flips on the trampoline—and a shiny blue ribbon (pinned onto a teddy bear) was the only thing she'd sleep with each night.

Here is her secret:

She'd do anything to get that fun back.

Anything.

DON'T DRIVE ANY FASTER THAN YOUR
GUARDIAN ANGEL CAN FLY.
—*Anonymous*

CLAIRE

Friday night, we're driving around—just my sister, Nellie, and me. It's almost June, and the air is damp with a mist flowing in from the bay. We're drinking iced coffee from Dunkin' Donuts, something that always tastes good, even after it's been sitting in a warm car for a while.

When I dare to let myself, this is how I remember what happened that night—like it's happening all over again.

My cell says 8:34. I'm waiting for Nick to call. There's supposed to be this rager on the beach. Three kegs. Can't wait.

But for the past ten minutes, all Nellie has done is play with the dial on the radio—changing stations, volume, bass. With two fingers on the wheel, not paying attention to the road, she seriously just blew through a stop sign.

"Whoopsy," she says.

"That's it," I tell her. "Pull over."

It's the end of my junior year, and I've been driving forever, unlike my ninth-grade sister, who's only had *her* permit for a few weeks. Thought I'd be nice and let her try some after-dark practice—but she is totally making me crazy.

"No, Claire. Please! Give me a break."

(Like life for her hasn't already been one huge, ginormous break.)

Should I let her keep driving—or not? Even if our mother's car happens to be an embarrassing, forest green station wagon—without anywhere to plug in my iPod—I'm responsible for bringing it home in one piece.

"Last chance," I tell her. "Stop messing around."

"Okay, *Dad*."

"This is me laughing," I reply. No smile, just a stare.

Usually I don't hang out with my sister on a Friday night, but our parents went to Boston to celebrate their anniversary. As owners of Perry's Sports, they don't get out much. Dad didn't want his precious baby stuck home alone—or out with me and my "older" friends.

Just to the movies and back, girls, he'd warned. Unlike Mom, he can be somewhat of a control freak.

I wasn't about to announce that I had no intention of wasting a perfectly good weekend night at the movies (or that I planned to let Nellie drive), but oh my god, the girl *obviously* needs practice—how else is she going to pass her road test? She can barely see over the wheel.

As I sip my coffee and glance in her direction, Nellie's hands are now perfectly positioned at ten and two. But then she takes another corner too wide—nearly hitting a man on his bike—and my foot almost goes through the floor!

"I didn't see him!" she cries. We've passed the guy, who's waving his arms and shouting obscenities, but unexpectedly, the next thing she does is step on the brakes . . . *hard*.

"What the—" My arm jerks back, and iced coffee spills all

over my white denim skirt. I take a napkin out of the paper bag and begin to wipe furiously—but now, *oh joy*, it's totally streaked with brown stains.

"That's it. You're finished. Look what you did."

"Sorry," she says lamely, pulling over to the side of the road.

I get out and go around to the driver's side, adjusting the seat for more leg room. Scooting over, she fumbles with her seat belt, cowering—as if I'd actually try to hit her. After a few minutes of my silent treatment, she reaches into her purse, takes out a hairbrush, and begins brushing her thick, straight, blonde hair. We're both half Irish, but luck didn't smile on me. I got stuck with not only *curly* but *red* hair (and a too-big butt from my mother's side).

"My favorite skirt is now ruined, thanks to you."

"I *said* I was sorry." She has the nerve to sound slightly indignant. "Are you going to be mad all night?"

Like I ever hold a grudge.

"You're not, right?" Her eyes sparkle, a golden topaz. "Can I drive again? Later?"

"Is that what we're calling it now? *Driving*?"

She laughs weakly. "Can I? On the way home?"

"Maybe. Possibly."

Who knows what condition I'll be in on the way home.

Jacob's Point, the road I've turned on, is in desperate need of a makeover, with ruts and potholes that bang and scrape the underside of the car. This completely annoys my father. Supposedly we pay a lot of taxes to live in Blair's Cove, Rhode Island, which is bordered by the Narragansett Bay on one side and the Three Mile River on the other. Our town has million-dollar water views and a competitive school district, but terrible, third-world-country-ish roads.

As we drive along, my sister points out the bright orb of a full moon rising over the bay. "Look at that moon! What a perfect night. Do you think Adam's there yet? I'm so glad you guys talked me into this. I love his sideburns. He has the most amazing smile."

"Really? I hadn't noticed."

That's not entirely true. My buddy Adam (or Fish, as his friends like to call him) has been making me and my best friend, Sid, smile since middle school. And he's lost a lot of weight recently. Like fifty pounds. Everyone's noticed that.

I follow her gaze out the window. The moon makes me think of the round chalk dish at the gym, which then reminds me: practice tomorrow morning. Seven a.m. on a Saturday morning. *Ugh*. How does Miss Perfect handle it six times a week?

(Note to self: backflips are not so much fun with a hangover.)

Honestly? *Nothing* is much fun with a hangover.

Okay, I admit, I've morphed into a regular "party girl" ever since I started going out with Nick last fall. At first it bothered me to lie and hide it from my parents, but lately it's become almost routine.

I've been to dozens of keggers with Nick, but I never dreamed of exposing my little sister—who has practically no social life outside the gym. But when I told my boyfriend a few days ago that I might not be able to come tonight because of Nellie, he didn't seem to understand.

"What's the problem, baby? Just bring her along."

"But I don't want to be the one to ruin her innocence!"

"It's bound to happen sooner or later," he argued. *"Look what happened to you."*

(For some reason, I winced inside when he said that.)

Afterward, when Sid and I were talking to Fish about the party, he got the biggest grin on his face. He thought Nellie could totally handle it.

Really?

Ever since the two of them "accidentally" wound up at the same movie together with their friends (a few weeks ago), I'd known that Nellie had a crush on Fish. But this was the first time I realized—yuck—that the feelings could be mutual. Adam Silva crushing on my little sister? That's borderline incestuous. But what could I do?

Anyway, Adam texted Nellie that he was planning to go tonight with Cookie and Kyle. But he had some other stuff to do first. Did she want to meet him at the party? Could she possibly drive with me?

So that's how it got decided. But I'm still not completely convinced she *can* handle it. "Remember, Nellie, when Mom asks, we went to the theater on Route 6."

"Je ne suis pas stupide," she replies with this annoyingly authentic-sounding accent.

My sister spent April vacation with our father at the Junior European Championships in Paris. Not that I'm jealous, but since then she's been acting like French is her second language or something.

"Well, don't go blabbing to all your little friends, either. I don't want Nick to get in trouble. Or Fish."

"You think I do?" she replies, and puts her coffee cup back into the cup holder. "Too many calories," she says. Like at a size 2 she really has to worry.

I take another sip of my drink, hitting mostly watery ice, just as my cell starts to chime. I flip it open. It's Nick.

"Hey, baby," he says. "What's going on?"

"Hey, yourself," I tell him. "Nothing. We've been driving around, waiting for you to call."

He tells me they're all set and that I should try to park on Lighthouse Lane. "But only if there's not a lot of other cars. And hurry up. I miss you."

"Okay. Miss you, too. Bye." I barely get the car turned around before my sister begins freaking out again.

"Did he say if Adam was there yet? What if he doesn't show? Are you sure Sid can't come?"

"Chill. I didn't ask. And, no, I told you about her teeth."

An orthodontic surgeon had to remove my best friend's impacted wisdom teeth yesterday, so there's no way she'd be up for a party. Still, Sid Mendoza tends to watch out for all of us when she's around—like a mother hen. I wish she was coming, too.

Nellie flips the visor, checks her lip gloss, and groans. "He's not going to be there. I just know it."

This is from Miss Level-9, who is state champion on vault and bars. (I prefer the beam because it's so precise, but I'm the sister who's destined to disappoint, I guess. I've never even qualified.)

"Do you seriously think he likes me?" Nellie whines.

Enough already!

"How the hell should I know? But don't act all desperate

when you see him. Boys hate that." This seems to shut her up—temporarily.

Lighthouse Lane is only about a five-minute drive away. When we get there, I park in front of a rambling old house that is completely dark inside, deserted-looking, and creepy.

Looking up the empty driveway, Nellie asks, "Are you sure this is right?"

"It's not a *house* party, Dense One. Remember? I told you, it's on the beach."

"Oh, right," she says, anxiously picking at her nail polish. "You know, I was thinking . . . maybe I'll wait in the car. Could you just text me if Adam's there?"

I shake my head in disgust. Why did I have a feeling she'd try to bail? "What's the matter with you, anyway? I thought you'd want to do something *normal* for a change."

"I do." She stares out the window. "It's just that Dad would flip out if he knew I went to a drinking party. Especially with Nationals only a month away."

I shoot her a glare. "Like he'd be thrilled to find out about me?"

"Of course not!"

But he wouldn't be *as* upset, and we both know it.

I sigh. "That's why Nick keeps the location a secret until the last minute. So we don't get caught by the police or whoever. Sometimes he even stashes the kegs in two different places— just in case."

"But what if we can't find it?"

I pat her leg. "Listen, it's easy. All we have to do is walk to the end of the street, get onto the beach, and follow the plastic cups."

She hesitates again. "But what if someone spikes my drink?"

"Look," I say, "nobody's going to spike your damn drink. You don't even have to drink at all."

She pauses to think that one over, but I notice she's no longer giving me any eye contact. "Don't be mad, okay? I think I'll just wait here."

Arggh!!! Why can't I have a normal sister like everyone else? Why do I have to be related to this neurotic, straight-edge gymnast *freak*?

Someone's got to give her a reality check.

"Do you really want to miss out on this? Not everyone gets gold, Nellie. Hardly anyone makes the national team. And they get injured, too. You, of all people, should know that. Can you imagine doing all of that hard work for nothing? Remember Samantha Peszek?"

No answer.

"Fine. Stay here. I hope it's worth it. I'm going to go have some fun."

With that, I get my jacket from the backseat, put the keys in my pocket, and slam the car door behind me. But as I walk down the desolate street to the beach, I can't resist the urge to glance back at my sister, a lonely silhouette in the car.

Oh my god. I refuse to feel guilty for leaving her. I refuse. (But I do.)

Fantastic.

What a frigging fantastic way to start the night.

CLAIRE

8:45 P.M. "Claire! Wait up!"

I hear the car door shut and watch as Nellie runs the few steps to catch up with me. "Sorry I freaked out just now," she explains. "I want to have fun. But I had this funny feeling. Like something bad was going to happen."

"What was it you used to call it?" I say, teasing. "ESPN?"

"Shut up." She laughs, taking my hand. "Let's go."

It always amazes me when we're walking together, how short my sister actually is: four-foot ten to my five-nine and a half. Because of my long legs, the top of her head barely grazes my shoulder. Sid tries to convince me that long legs are sexy, but they're not very practical for a gymnast. Oh, they might look great straddling the beam, but those dismounts will jack you up every time.

We leave the street for a narrow, grassy trail where every so often we get a glimpse of the water. After we climb over the last few rocks, the shimmering bay seems to open up in front of us—like a present—stretching clear to the horizon.

"There's one!" Nellie says excitedly, pointing at a red cup lying on a pile of dried seaweed.

"See, I told you. It must be this way."

As we walk along, tiny shells and mollusks crunch under our feet. In the distance the blurry lights of the Newport Bridge glow like a necklace though the mist. And there, up ahead of us: the party!

About forty or so kids are hanging out on the beach, standing around a smoky driftwood fire. When we get closer, Nick's friends (and a few boys I don't know) say hi to me. Being the party host's girlfriend brings with it a certain degree of status, I guess. But at the same time—and I don't think this is my imagination—they seem to be eagerly checking out my little sister.

As I look around, I'm annoyed that Meredith (Nick's ex) has made it here before me again. She's with bleached-blonde Gabby and stuck-up Kristen. The three of them seem to think they're popular, but nobody actually likes them.

Nellie pulls at my arm. "I don't see Adam yet, do you?"

"He said he'd be here. Stop stressing. You could always talk to Meredith," I tell her. "Look, there's Nick."

My boyfriend strolls over and picks me up off the ground in a powerful, rib-crushing hug. A hockey jersey (B.U. in the fall) hangs over his faded jean shorts. From this angle, all I can see are his hairy legs and gigantic feet in his brown leather Birkies. "Put me down, you crazy person!"

Nick holds on for just a minute longer, then he French-kisses me hello. There's a lock of hair in his eyes, so I brush it away.

"What took you so long?" he says.

I smile back, thinking he probably missed me. Or not. I watch as his eyes visibly widen at Nellie, who's quietly standing beside me.

"Hey, Nick," she says, glancing up at him.

Sid and I like to tease my sister because she took forever to develop (elite-level gymnasts usually do), but now with a chill in the air, her short denim skirt, and that snug white camisole top—well, she doesn't look like my *little* sister anymore.

"Hey, sexy," he replies.

I punch him on the arm. "That's my sister, pervert."

He turns red and squirms. "Don't be like that, baby." He puts his hands on either side of my face and kisses me again, sweetly this time.

"You taste so good," he murmurs, and those blue, bedroom eyes almost manage to change my mood.

"Well, you *so* taste like beer." I glance over at where they're keeping the kegs. "Go get me some, okay?"

His hand grazes the side of my hip. "Only if you promise to stay right here. I mean it, *woman*. You're with me tonight."

As we watch him lumber away behind a sand dune, I'm thinking maybe things *will* be okay between us tonight. But then, of course, I'm forgetting about Meredith, who comes out from behind that very same dune a few minutes later.

"Want one?" She's holding two red cups against her impossibly flat stomach, one in each hand. She's almost too thin, if you ask me. But I'm happy that her black hair (longish, side-part) is frizzy from the humidity—just like mine.

"Nick said to tell you he'll be right back," Meredith says. "They're having trouble with the spigot. So, um, don't be mad at him, Claire."

"Oh, definitely. I won't be mad because *you* said not to," I reply.

Unfortunately, she's too busy staring at my coffee-stained skirt to register my sarcasm. "Hey, is that supposed to be retro tie-dyed, or what?"

"Or what," I say. I glare at Nellie and take a sip of beer. As usual, it tastes cool and bitter going down. I'm about to take another when the most surprising thing happens—my little sister grabs the cup from me.

"*Merci*," she replies, gulping it fast. She doesn't give it back, either—not even when I hold out my hand. "Is it okay, Claire?" she asks, wiping off a mustache of foam.

"Not really," I say, because there goes my buzz. Yet for once in her life, she's acting seminormal. "No, whatever, it's fine. I'll drive later. But slow down, there's plenty."

"I know," she says, giggling. "I was chugging it!"

Meredith raises an eyebrow. "And you were worried about her fitting in? By the way, did you hear Fish brought over the kegs when R.J.'s boat wouldn't start? I'm surprised his old putt-putt made it across the cove. Look, there he is now."

"Yay!" says Nellie. "I think he's so cute."

"Cute?" Meredith rolls her eyes. "Maybe in a flabby sort of way. Haven't you noticed he kinda smells? You can do much better, Nellie."

My sister waves Fish over to us. I actually like the way Adam's new "metrosexual" sideburns run down his jawline. And with his shirt tucked into his cargo shorts, he's definitely not hiding behind fat clothes anymore.

"Hey, Adam," says Nellie, grinning.

"What's up, Fish?" says Meredith, instantly all fake-nice.

"Same old," he replies, nudging into my sister. "Kegstands

started early. Now it's time for crab-ball, apparently."

On the beach behind him, a group of guys are tossing the helmet-like shell of a dead horseshoe crab into the air and batting at it with a stick. One of the guys, Trevor, keeps falling over drunk. Lying on his side, he smacks the shell straight into the fire, where it pops and burns. Then he vomits on somebody's shoe.

"Good one!" Adam yells, clapping. "He's so fried."

"Thanks again for transporting our beverages," Meredith says, as if it were *her* boyfriend's party or something.

"Yeah," I add quickly. "That was cool."

"Oooh! That's right," Nellie says. "Your boat's here. Can I have a ride?" She's standing on tiptoe, looking around. "Where is it? I can't see."

"That's 'cause you can't see much of anything down there," he replies. "Here, let me help." He lifts her up by the waist somewhat awkwardly.

"Don't!" she protests, but of course she loves the attention.

"Actually," he explains, quickly putting her down, "my boat's already home, safe at our dock. Couldn't risk the rocks tearing it up in low tide. I came back here in my car with Cookie and Kyle. I'm the D.D. tonight."

Behind us there are more shouts and laughter. I turn to see Pete, another hockey player, head-butt Nick in the stomach. So *there's* my boyfriend. They roll around on the soft sand, play-wrestling together.

When the boys stand up and brush themselves off, Nick doesn't come back to me like I thought he would. Instead, after a minute, I see the flame of a lighter and then a familiar smell mingles with the smoke from the fire.

So much for Nick's promises to quit smoking weed.

"Boys will be boys," Meredith observes smugly.

Ugh, I wish Sid were here. Sid always gives good advice on bad boyfriend behavior. While Fish and Nellie are talking, I'm busy trying to pretend that Nick's antics aren't bothering me. Then a few minutes later, R.J., the giant of the hockey team, marches past us with a stack of pizza boxes balanced against his chest.

"Food!" he yells. "Who the hell wants food?"

My dad would say he's got "bricks for brains," but I have to put up with him because he's Nick's best friend.

We watch R.J. head down the beach, and then Meredith taps my sister. "Claire and I don't need the calories, Nellie, but do you want a slice before it's gone?"

Hate, hate, *hate* her.

"Maybe," Nellie says, hesitating. "Do you guys mind?"

"Why would they mind?" Meredith insists. "Come with me. Just for a few minutes. And I'll show you where we go pee, if you have to, behind this old rowboat."

Nellie glances at Adam, checking if it's okay with him.

"It's fine," he says, smiling. "Bring me back some, okay?"

Meredith never misses an opportunity to act superior. She arches an eyebrow. "You want some of her, um, *pee*?"

It works. He's flustered. "Pizza. You *knew* what I meant."

"Just kidding," she replies. "So sensitive."

After they wander off in R.J.'s direction, I say, "Wow. Is there anything more fun than hanging out with Meredith?"

"Hmm. Let me think." Adam pauses. "Getting a penis tattoo?"

"Oh, god."

"Or what about a nipple piercing?"

"Stop," I say, grinning. "You're so bad."

Fish keeps bashing Meredith until he makes me laugh so hard, I'm in tears. But twenty minutes later Nick is *still* getting wasted behind us—along with half the hockey team. What happened to him being only with me tonight?

I guess it must show on my face, because Adam nods over his shoulder and says, "Not that it's any of my business, but he's so unworthy."

"Excuse me?"

"I don't know, Claire. It's like you're way up high, on this towering marble parapet overlooking . . . whatever. And Nick's just a flea on the sand." He squints like he's examining a pretend bug between two fingers, and then deliberately flicks it away.

"Parapet? Cool. But a *flea*? Really? You couldn't come up with anything better than that?" I start laughing again anyway.

"I could," he says, shrugging. "Don't think you'd want to hear it."

I roll my eyes. He's right about one thing, though. The way Nick is acting tonight, he doesn't deserve me.

The surf, which was rough and insistent when we first got here, seems to have settled down. I'm thinking Adam will want to go rescue Nellie, but surprisingly he stays.

"So, are you or Sid working this summer?" he asks casually. "Or Nellie?"

Fish's summer job is digging for clams—that's what it's been since he moved here in seventh grade. Quahogging can be hot, smelly, and backbreaking work. He also helps out on his dad's fishing boat, which is 1) where he got his nickname, 2) why he has to go heavy on the Axe spray, and 3) what Meredith was nastily referring to before.

"Sid's working at the ice-cream shop in Bristol," I tell him. "I'll be teaching cartwheels this summer. But my sister? Are you serious? Not with her knee finally healed. She'll be obsessively practicing for Nationals. She was too young for Beijing, but she's a rising star. My father pushes us hard."

I think for a minute and correct myself. "Nellie, anyway. I guess he's finally given up on me."

Adam sighs and scratches his chin. "Lucky you. Pop likes to bust my chops all the time."

I frown. "It's not like he loves her more or anything."

Why am I telling him this?

Fish moves a little closer and lowers his voice. "No. He probably just loves you different—that's all."

Strange, my heart kind of skips a beat when he says that.

Just then a glow-in-the-dark Frisbee lands at our feet. Adam bends over to pick it up. Jason (from trig class) is standing ankle-deep in water near the shoreline. "Hey, Fish! Are you playing or what?"

His friends, Kyle and Cookie, are waiting there, too. They're on the JV lacrosse team, which hasn't won a game all season.

Adam tosses the Frisbee back to them. "Listen, I'm gonna go. When you see your sister, tell her I'll be over there. Maybe she forgot I was hungry?" He shakes his head, smiling. "*Girls.*"

"Okay, well, it was good to—"

Then another voice interrupts behind me. "*Claire?*"

"Nick?"

"Fish!" yells Kyle. "Come *on*!"

Adam tries to go around us to join them, but Nick sticks out an elbow, blocking his way.

"Hold on there, Fish-man." He's got a blanket under his arm and a beer in each hand. We wait as he sets down the foamy cups, twisting them into the sand. "Everything okay here, baby?"

"Why wouldn't it be?"

"Good question." Nick stares at Adam, red-eyed. "I just heard you took your boat back, dude. One of the kegs is busted. How the hell are we supposed to return it?"

Adam shrugs, glancing at me. "Well, nobody told me that. Anyway, it's low tide. I can't take any chance with the rocks and all. My boat is like my job."

Nick puffs himself up all intimidating. "Still a problem, bro."

Fish is shaking his head. "Yeah, well, actually, not *my* problem." He gives my shoulder a gentle squeeze. "Later, Claire." And begins to walk away.

"Yeah, *much* later," Nick replies. His eyes are narrow, jealous slits. "Why is that freak always hitting on you?"

"Fish? Are you serious? Actually, Nellie thinks she likes him."

"That's a reach." Nick acts surprised. "For *him*." Then he adds, overly loud, "Fat freak has a bad attitude!"

"Shut up, Nick," I say, embarrassed. I punch his arm, but he barely flinches. "In case you haven't noticed, he's not—"

"Fat anymore?" Nick laughs, interrupting me, and says even louder, "Yeah, but he's still a freak."

Adam glances back, overhearing us, crushed.

Trying to smooth it over, I wave at him. "Bye. See you later? Okay?"

Nick grumbles. "Why encourage the mud raker?"

So ridiculous! Poor Adam. Nellie should be back here by now. I open my cell to check the time. It's after nine. I scan the beach. *Where the hell did she go?*

CLAIRE

9:15 P.M. Nick pulls me down next to him on the blanket. I pick up a broken seashell and run my finger along the sharp edge. He starts kissing me, but I'm not into kissing him back. And when he tries to slide his hand up under my shirt, I push his hand away. We go back and forth like that for a while.

"Come on, baby. What's wrong?"

"I just don't feel like it." Not when he's high.

He sulks. I fume. About ten minutes later, my sister returns.

"Hey, there you guys are." She flops down on the blanket, fanning herself exaggeratedly. With her legs apart like that, I can practically see up her skirt. "It's so darn hot. Don't you think so, Claire?"

Hot?

I'm thinking no, it's definitely *not* hot. The wind has changed direction, and it's blowing cool air off the bay. Besides, everybody knows that summer doesn't happen till July (if we're lucky) in New England.

"How was your pizza?" I say, not really caring. "Took you long enough."

"Okay. Kind of greasy. Are you mad at me, Claire?" I can't help noticing that her eyes are shiny like glass.

"Why?" I shrug. "Should I be?"

"No. But guess what?" She kicks off her sneakers and sinks her toes in the sand. "We were just doing Jell-O shots! Did you ever do a Jell-O shot? Meredith had them in a cooler."

What the hell? Meredith had my little sister doing *shots*?!

"Well, you should try one sometime. They're yummy." Then she leans over, distracted, looking for something in her purse. "Can you check my phone, Claire? It keeps beeping. R.J. is coming back for me in a second." She hands it to me.

I put it down next to mine, but I'm thinking, *R.J.?* What about Adam? Has she forgotten all about him already? Before he even had a chance?

"Fish was looking for you, Nellie. You kind of ditched him."

Her eyes glaze over. "He was? I did? Oh."

R.J. comes up to us then, staggering slightly. For a giant, he's got what Sid calls a "pinhead" on a long swan neck. He's also tall enough that if he toppled over he could really hurt you—so I quickly get out of his way.

Nellie jumps up from the blanket. He steadies himself by putting his hands around her waist. "You ready, little Nells? How about a few flips?"

Little Nells?

"Should I, Claire?" she asks. "Somebody saw that article about me in the newspaper. They want me to do one of our routines."

"Go for it," says Nick.

Are they serious? They want her to do a routine now? When she's half wasted on a rocky beach?

"I don't think so. Couldn't they just come to one of our meets?" I say.

"Of course they *could*, baby," Nick replies, all patronizing. "But I think R.J. wants to see her *now*."

R.J. nods and slaps him a high-five. "Thanks, bro. That I do."

My sister tucks in her cami and ties back her hair. Before I can stop her, she's halfway up the beach, searching for a flat stretch of sand.

"You better hope she doesn't get hurt," I warn them, because if she does, I will seriously have to kill them both.

"She won't," says R.J., blowing me off. "I love to see chicks do splits and stuff."

"Seriously, Claire," Nick mutters. "You worry too much."

A bunch of kids have gathered behind us to watch. Nellie puts her hands on her hips; she has this look of intense concentration on her face. She gets into a sprinting position, calf muscles twitching, up on her toes.

Ready. Set. She takes a long running start. A front handspring leads into a cartwheel and then a round-off. Having seen her do this routine so many times, I practically know it by heart. A gainer back walkover, an aerial cartwheel, and then a split. Four lightning-fast backflips in a row.

She is so fast! Pure energy. Even if I practiced every day for the next thousand years, I'd never be as good. Or as airheaded. My oblivious sister doesn't seem to mind that everyone is getting a glimpse of her pink high-cut underwear every time she goes over—but I do.

People are clapping, Nick is whistling, and R.J. clumsily spills his beer on my shirt. "Your sister is so frigging hot!"

Next to me, I overhear Chris Hawkins rating her body parts. "Nice legs. Great hair. Outstanding ass."

I groan. Is this how it's going to be for the rest of high school?

They are such pigs! But—and, I hate myself for this—I sort of wish (somewhere deep inside), that they were saying that about *me*.

All of a sudden, R.J. positions himself right where my sister's about to land after her next move. "Come over here, sexy," he says. "You're making me horny." He lunges and tries to catch her.

At first Nellie manages to get past him, but his legs are much longer. He scoops her up quickly. With her feet hanging down around his knees, it's like she's his own personal toy doll.

"No, I'm not finished," she says loudly. "I want to show them the rest. Stop. *Stop!*" She's kicking his shins. "Put me down!"

But R.J. is all worked up. He doesn't want to stop. His face is on her neck, his hips are grinding into her, and his hands are pushing up her skirt and grabbing at her butt. *Predator!*

I start to march over, about to put an end to it, when out of nowhere Adam shows up—and he looks *pissed*.

"Didn't she ask you to put her down?" He twists R.J.'s arm, and Nellie slips away and rushes over to me.

"Next time try listening," Adam says, disgusted.

R.J. opens his mouth in a look of fake surprise. "Why are you even still *here,* man? Shouldn't you be at a Weight Watchers meeting or something?" Then he doubles over at his own joke. It's not really that funny, but some of the other kids are laughing, too.

Nick slaps his thigh, roaring. "Oh, hell. You schooled him!"

That's when, without any warning, Adam makes a fist, pulls back his arm, and aims high. I can't believe it.

It's a lucky shot, because R.J. stumbles once, then falls flat on his back. He lies there a minute, rubbing his chin—stunned. I don't think Fish can believe it, either.

Beside me, Nick is totally flipping out. "What the—?"

Things get very scary then, very fast. Nick tosses his cup to the side and charges across the beach. Unaware, Adam has his back to us, walking away, when Nick power-slams him to the ground from behind, like he's checking somebody at a hockey game. Adam crumples, facedown, in the sand.

But apparently that's not enough. Nick's fists begin flying at Adam's head and his shoulders. Fish manages to roll over and tries to fight back, but it's useless; Nick pummels him again and again.

"What are you doing!?" I scream. "Stop it, Nick! Get off him!"

Nick acts like he can't hear me—or if he does, he doesn't care. Then R.J. scrambles up, so now it's two against one.

"Yeah! Yeah!" people yell as all chaos breaks out.

I'm so shocked. I've never seen Nick attack anyone before—much less one of my friends. Finally, Kyle and Cookie push their way in. They grab onto R.J.'s shirt and hold him back—but Nick is like this out-of-control machine; he keeps punching Adam, over and over.

Nellie cries out, "No! You're hurting him, *please!*"

At last, enough guys muscle in and drag Nick off. Adam is still on the ground, breathing hard. There is a thin line of blood dripping out of his nose and a layer of sand on his clothes, along his arms, and in his hair.

After a few seconds Adam lifts his head. "I'm all right," he says to Kyle. "I'll be okay." One of his eyes is puffy and he's got a fat lip, but considering how hard Nick was punching him, I guess it could be worse.

Cookie offers his hand. "Man, I thought he was gonna—"

"I said, I'm *okay,*" Adam repeats, forcefully this time. Trying to regain some dignity, he stands up, brushes himself off, and wipes his nose on his sleeve.

When things have settled down, and the crowd breaks up, Adam comes over to check on us. "We're bouncing. Are you girls all right? Anybody hurt?"

"We're fine," I say, although my sister's a sniveling mess.

"Call me later?" she begs, hanging onto his arm. "Please?"

He shrugs. "Whatever. I guess."

"Just let go of him, Nellie," I say before she humiliates herself any further. What a frigging nightmare! I refuse to stay a minute longer. "Go get our phones, Nellie. We're done, too."

"Okay." She heads toward the blanket.

Nick gazes in my direction. "What're you doing?" He seems to be having trouble focusing. "Don't go yet, baby. What'sa matter?"

"Shut up, Nick." I want to tell him off so badly, but I can't even stand to be near him. I start to follow Nellie to speed her along, but of course I don't get very far before I feel this tugging on the back of my shirt, almost like I'm stuck on something. (Something pathetic and idiotic and wasted.)

"Claire. Wait. You saw the whole thing. What'd I do wrong?" Nick never gives up easily.

Turning around, I give him one of my best ice-queen stares. "Really, Nick? Fish was only trying to help. I mean, R.J. was practically molesting my sister."

Nick shakes his head, laughing. "Nah! You know R.J. He was jus' playing." Then his eyes turn flat and mean. "Besides, that freak started it. You saw him. Fish totally hammered the first punch."

"Even if that's true, did you almost have to kill him?"

"But I didn't," he says, like that's something to be proud of. "Did I?"

"No. You're awesome. Way to go, hero."

"Don't be like that." His voice softens, trying to garner some sympathy from me. "What was I supposed to do, baby? Not help one of my friends?"

"Who *are* you?" I shake my head, incredulous. *Nothing* is ever his fault. "I'm not sure we belong together anymore."

"What? Tha's crazy. Yes, we do. Come here." He grips my wrist so hard that it actually hurts. "Don't go yet. Please. I need you."

"But I don't need you," I suddenly realize, and I twist and pull away from him.

CLAIRE

9:45 P.M. "I just texted Adam," Nellie says as we walk back to our car. "He didn't answer. Do you think he's mad at me?"

"Well, I don't think he's too happy with either of us at the moment."

"It's all my fault," she says dejectedly.

"Not completely," I say, although she did more than her share to contribute to that crazy fight, having to be Miss Center of Attention—like always.

The dozen or so cars and small SUVs that were parked near us are pulling away, with their radios so loud the cars are practically vibrating. It's unanimous: party officially *over*.

We get into my mother's station wagon, and as I put the key into the ignition, I'm glad I only had a few sips of beer. Our house isn't far away, just a few miles. "Still want to drive?" I ask my sister.

"Not funny," she says, slumping down in the seat.

I head up Lighthouse and turn onto Jacob's Point. It's wooded and dark on this road with no streetlights—and all of those annoying potholes. After I hit a particularly nasty one, my sister holds her stomach and groans.

"If I tell you to stop, Claire, do it, okay? I think I might be sick."

I study her face. "Are you drunk . . . or what?"

"Maybe . . . I don't know. My head feels dizzy. I think those shots just hit me." She leans back against the headrest and closes her eyes. Suddenly my phone rings, and she glances at me. I look to see who it is, then toss it on the floor without answering.

"Adam?" she asks, hopefully.

"No, Nick. Not talking to him."

She nods. "That's good. I didn't realize he was such a—"

"Complete and total psycho? Me neither. I'm breaking up with him."

My sister makes a face like she's heard that before. "But you *never*—"

"First thing tomorrow," I say, interrupting. "So shut up."

(I don't tell her this, but I'm hoping this time, he'll let me.)

Outside my car windows, crickets are chirping in the fields, and the moon is smaller and high in the sky. The road twists and turns here along the river. When I round the next curve, I notice we're directly behind a black Nissan Maxima. The license plates read: 4-CLAMS. *Adam's* car.

"Oh, look," Nellie says, excited. "I can't believe we caught up with him already. Maybe he was driving extra slow."

"Well, he probably had to drop off Cookie and Kyle."

She grins. "Could you speed up and get next to his car?"

On this road? Is she crazy?

"Come on," she pleads. "I want to make sure he's okay."

"We just saw him, Nellie. He's fine."

At least I'm hoping Adam will *be* fine, eventually. Actually, I'm feeling semiresponsible for what happened tonight. Not that it's my job to control my soon-to-be ex-boyfriend's behavior, but it's so beyond wrong what Nick did.

Nellie starts again. "We owe it to him, Claire."

The road is straightening out here a little. "Okay," I relent, although I've never passed a car before. Not on a two-lane road, anyway. A bead of sweat gathers and drips from under my arm. Glancing in the rearview, I put on my turn signal and press the gas.

Fish slows down when he realizes it's us, so that's good.

When we're close enough, Nellie leans out the window. "Woo-hoo!" she yells. "Hope you're not mad!" Then she laughs—this crazy dumb laugh.

Another car is approaching, so I quickly pull back behind him again.

"What is your problem?" I say, so annoyed with her now. "I thought you were sorry."

"I don't know." She sinks into her seat. "Sometimes I laugh when I'm nervous."

Ahead of us, Adam slows down more and sticks his arm out of the car window. He's giving us two fingers for the "peace" sign, so maybe he's not too pissed off. But then the two fingers become one, and he's flipping us the bird!

As he roars ahead, there's a blast of exhaust coming out of his tailpipe.

"Oh, no." Nellie runs her hand through her hair, which is a windblown mess. "Do you think that means he's upset?"

"Well, let's see. First, you ditch him at the party. Then, he gets beat up trying to help you. And just now, you were laughing at him. It doesn't take a brain surgeon to figure that out."

Nellie sighs. "Poor Adam."

I'm suddenly outraged. "He doesn't deserve to be treated that way!"

"I know . . . but,"—she looks at me strangely—"nothing's hap'ning between the two of you, right? I mean if it was . . . if you were . . . I would never . . ." She's acting so goofy, actually slurring her words.

"Don't be crazy. We're just friends."

"Good. Then I know how to make him feel better." She leans over and gives me a big, sloppy hug. "Catch up and pass him, again, 'kay? Love ya. You're the best."

Sure. Fine. I'm the best. Except for when I'm not.

(Like every frigging day of my life.)

I keep driving, my eyes on the road, trying to ignore my sister, but when I take the next sharp curve, she falls over sideways, almost landing in my lap. She's laughing hysterically now—totally drunk off her ass. I notice Adam's car is right in front of us again.

"Put your seat belt back on. You're going to get us hurt!"

Why is she making me act like our mother?

"I will. In a minute. First I'm going to *flash* him. It'll be so much fun, Claire. Meredith said she does it to boys all the time."

Wonderful. Now skanky Meredith is her role model.

Nellie giggles. "And tell him I love him, too. He deserves to know. After all he's been through for me tonight."

I shake my head. "You are seriously wasted."

She kneels on the front seat, with her camisole looped around her neck. "Pass him, Claire! Pass him *now,* okay? Beep your horn!"

Looking back, this is exactly when I should've taken a deep

breath, slowed down, and pulled over. But for some reason I didn't.

Maybe it's because I was pissed at Meredith for giving Nellie those shots in the first place.

Or maybe I was disgusted that I stayed with a boyfriend like Nick for so long.

Or maybe, I was never the "nice" sister. I guess all those years of playing second best had finally caught up with me.

∞

Nellie is already practically hanging out of the window, her boobs exposed.

"Woo-hoo!" she yells. "LOVE YOU!"

Honestly? Right now a part of me is hoping, if I *do* pass Adam, he'll think my sister is being an immature idiot—or maybe even a slut. So I decide to give her *exactly* what she's asking for. If she's determined to make a complete and utter fool of herself, who am I to stand in her way?

"Okay, you asked for it," I say, pulling out to pass. "Here we go."

She's still leaning out the window as the front bumper of my car edges up next to the driver's door of Adam's car. That's when I see the headlights coming toward me, on the side I'm passing on. Bright headlights. High beams flashing. The car isn't far off.

I definitely can't get around Adam now, so I slow down until Nellie's side window is even with his back fender. But when I glance in my rearview so I can pull back into the lane behind him, there's *another* set of headlights.

What the hell? As we rounded that last curve, another car must have sped up and eased in behind Adam's car!

"Nellie, get back in here."

The car approaching us is getting closer and closer. And the jerk-off behind Adam won't give up any room. But Fish can't speed ahead, either, because there's a car in front of him. The road was empty a minute ago!

"Where did all these damn cars come from?" I glance nervously at my sister, taking my eyes—for just a split second— off the road.

"What are you doing?!" Nellie screams, grabbing the wheel. "He's going to hit us!"

That's when I must have panicked. Panicked and stepped on the gas.

I steer hard to the left to get out of the way, and the approaching car flies past us, horn blasting. I'm about to pull back into the right lane when—*shit!*—I hit a pothole, more like a crater, and Nellie falls forward on top of me. All I can feel are her elbows—or are those her knees?—jabbing into my side.

"Get off me!" I yell. But as I try to push her off, I suddenly lose control of the car. Instantly we are flying off the road, over the curb, into the dirt, and through the trees. *This can't be happening.* Vines and branches are thwacking against the windshield blocking my view.

Oh, my god, I'm thinking, *I can't see!*

As we careen through the woods and down an embankment, I hear the sound of someone screaming.

My screaming? Nellie's screaming? It doesn't last long.

Because we crash. Into *something*. A tree? I think it's a tree.

We crash with a horribly loud crack, and the airbag

inflates and pushes into my face, but at least we're not moving anymore. After all of that, the car has

Finally

Stopped

Moving

And I'm alive, or at least I think I'm alive, and we're okay, or at least I think we're okay, but I can't see a thing. And when I ask, "Nellie? Are you all right? Are you okay?"

No reply. Nothing.

"Nellie!" I shout, but she doesn't answer. What if she's hurt? What if she's *dead*? No, she's not dead! She *can't* be dead!

There is an eerie quiet. Not the chirping of crickets or the wind rustling through the trees. It's a deathly, world-stopping silence.

That's the last thing I remember: the silence.

ONE GOOD THING ABOUT MUSIC,
WHEN IT HITS YOU, YOU FEEL NO PAIN.
—BOB MARLEY

ADAM

My father uses his hands for unloading crates, pulling the bull rake, or shucking clams. His hands are hugely muscular, almost cartoonishly big, with dark blue veins that snake from his wrists and across his tendons in thick, wavelike ridges. He also works commercial fishing boats when we're running low on funds. Anyway, his hands are what I'm staring at as he signs the papers releasing me into his custody.

"Got everything, Adam?" Officer Burton asks. The front desk at the police station is dark and empty. Everyone has left for the night.

"Yeah, thanks."

I pick up my iPod, wallet, phone, and keys and follow my dad through the dimly lit parking lot, to his decrepit white truck with the back bumper that is actually a wooden two-by-four. The nets and clam hoes (and everything else) are all heaped in the truck bed.

He opens the passenger door. After pushing aside some empty coffee cups and old newspapers, I climb in. I barely get started checking my messages when he grabs my phone. "I'll take that," he says. "And you're grounded. Until further notice."

"You're not giving me a chance to explain?"

No answer. I don't push. He lights a cigarette.

Pop's hair is pulled back into a thinning ponytail under a faded red baseball hat. He drives extra slowly out of the police station, to the end of the street. The whole time he doesn't say another word to me about being arrested. Nothing. Nada. It's kind of freaking me out.

Then he stops at the parking lot behind the all-night convenience store. We just sit there. I'm thinking maybe we need milk or bread or something?

It's probably in my best interest to talk. "I'll go in if you want, Pop. But I need some money first."

"Money? You want money?" Unexpectedly, he slaps me on the back of my head. *Not* gently.

"What the hell, Dad?"

"There won't be any money left after I pay your goddamn legal fees. Transporting alcohol to minors," he says. "Across state lines! What were you thinking?"

"I guess I wasn't," I reply angrily, rubbing out the sting.

"Thought I raised you better. If your mother was here . . ."

I don't remember my father ever hitting me, my whole entire life; he didn't have to. He's a Vietnam vet, original hard-ass. I learned years ago how to avoid pissing him off. (And he never hit my mother, either; that's not why she left.)

"But she isn't here," I say with an attitude. "And neither were you. I was locked up in there half the night. Like a common criminal!"

"Sorry," he says guiltily, as he flicks off an ash. "Nobody said you were a criminal. You know we're always late pulling into the dock. Besides, I spent a few hours in jail myself, around your age. Helped clear my head."

I'm about to say—*Yeah, well, I'm not you*—but why risk another pounding? Besides, maybe my head *did* need some clearing.

My father hacks then spits out the window. "But what made you do something so crazy, Adam? You've never let me down before. What the hell happened?"

"I don't know. I'm not sure. See, there was this party, and . . ."

I give him just enough to keep him satisfied and tell him how sorry I am (which is true), and after I'm finished, he starts the car and we drive home in silence, with me listening to Marley on my iPod and Dad puffing away on his cigs. I only hope Claire and Nellie are gonna be okay. They've *got* to be okay.

After my father goes to bed, I bum a smoke from the pack he always leaves on the counter—'cause I've never needed one more in my life. I grab my phone and some matches from his jacket pocket and ease the screen door behind me so it doesn't bang.

As I walk to our dock, the long, wet grass makes my ankles itch. It's low tide, but the saltwater river is turning, and the full moon bounces off the current like an interrogation lamp. I sit down on the wooden planks. Balancing the cigarette between my fingers, I strike a match and take a drag . . . and practically cough up a lung.

It's been a while since I quit smoking. With my throat still on fire, I toss the butt into the river, where it floats next to my clamming boat (not much bigger than a rowboat), which is fitted with an outboard motor and a small square cabin at the bow. Three years ago I bought this old skiff with the money I made helping my dad on his.

Was it only a few hours ago I was tearing across the river with three kegs rolling around on the deck behind me? Like such the big man. *I can hook you up, Nick*, I'd offered when I'd seen them at the gas station. *Don't cancel the party.* Why did I ever agree to help that tool?

Simple. 'Cause Nellie was going to be there—and Claire.

Claire . . . I had been having so much fun talking with her on the beach, just the two of us, before everything got messed up. How could things get so messed up? This is the worst night of my life.

No, I take that back. But it's the second worst, anyway.

I can't seem to figure out what part of this is my fault. Like seeing R.J. with his hands all over Nellie. Would things have turned out differently if I'd just walked away? Or what if I hadn't asked Nellie to meet me there in the first place? Would she have gone anyway? With Claire?

How much of that accident is because of me?

Did I mention that I actually saw their car spin off the road? One minute their headlights were bright in my rearview mirror . . . and the next?

I've never been the first person at the scene of an accident before. Their car was an accordion, no hood left at all. Nellie's body was inside, pinned to the dash. I couldn't tell if she was alive or . . .

So, I immediately called 911. *Head injuries bleed a lot.* That's what the EMT told me after I helped Claire out of the car. *Stay with them, okay? Don't move the other girl. Stay right there.*

Did he really think I was the kind of kid who would even *consider* leaving them? That was the *last* thing on my mind. My exact thoughts were: *Nellie can't be dead. Stay close to Claire. Tell her Nellie will be okay. Try to believe it.*

Actually, that's not one-hundred-percent true. When I was crouched there on the damp ground, holding Claire—the main weird/crazy thought that entered my head was: *I don't ever want to let this girl go.*

"Nellie thought you were upset," Claire told me in between her sobbing and weeping. "She wanted to make sure you were all right."

Was that why they were trying to pass me?

Hearing that made me feel a thousand times worse.

Almost as bad as when the police officer started eyeing me all suspicious as he was writing up the accident report. "Do you know these girls? Have they been drinking? Where did they get the alcohol?"

"I'm not sure," I replied as the ambulance drove away. "Can we talk about it some other time? I'm seriously freaked out right now."

"No, I don't think so, pal."

At the police station, Detective Burton didn't miss a thing. "Where did you get the black eye, son? We heard there was a party. Who was there? You know what happens if you're caught withholding information, right?"

So, with the tape recorder running, I told him everything that happened, and then I started naming names. "But not everyone there was drinking."

"Take it easy," he interrupted. "If we press charges, we

only need to know who supplied the alcohol. You say you brought it over in your boat. Do you know who purchased the kegs?"

"Nick Fronchetta. A kid named Chris Hawkins, and R.J. Lyons."

"You're doing the right thing," the detective assured me. "It can be hard for some kids to turn in their friends."

Friends? I pictured Nick's fist connecting with my face and all the other things he's said or done.

Flabb-o.

Do you smell something fishy?

Fat freak has a bad attitude.

The detective said he'd keep what I said confidential, at least for now. Then he turned me over to a female clerk with gray wispy hair who typed up my statement so I could sign it and go home.

"Where's your mom at?" she asked. "We're about done here."

"She moved away. Six years ago. Arizona."

(*With her d.bag boyfriend*, I might have added—but didn't.)

"And so you don't have to ask, my father is fishing past Point Judith. That's his job. He won't be back till late. Real late."

The lady frowned. "Well, we can't release you except to a parent."

All of that was hours ago. I can't help stressing, is Claire okay? Will Nellie make it through the night? And now, sitting on the dock, staring at the moon on the water, I realize I probably need to talk to someone—or maybe I just need to cry. I haven't cried since I was a little kid, but believe me there have been plenty of sad times in my life when I probably *should* have.

But it's two-thirty in the goddamn morning. Who's even awake to talk *to*? Cookie and Kyle have a lacrosse game tomorrow, so I know they're asleep. What other best friends do I have?

Then it hits me—Sid probably hasn't found out about the accident yet. I can't let her hear about it from somebody else.

But when I open my cell to call her, I see a new message. A text from Nellie. She must have sent it right before . . .

And then my mind immediately goes to: *What if it's the last one she ever sends me?* I read it first, and then, screw *not* crying, 'cause it says:

DON'T BE MAD! LOVE U! SEE U SOON!

THE RISK OF INJURY IN GYMNASTICS INCLUDES MINOR
INJURIES, SUCH AS BRUISES, AND SERIOUS INJURIES, SUCH
AS BROKEN BONES, DISLOCATIONS, AND MUSCLE PULLS.
UNFORTUNATELY, AS IN PRACTICALLY EVERY SPORT,
THE RISK ALSO INCLUDES VERY SERIOUS INJURIES, SUCH
AS PERMANENT PARALYSIS OR EVEN DEATH FROM
LANDINGS OR FALLS ONTO THE BACK, NECK, OR HEAD.
—*Make the Team*

NELLIE'S BRAIN

I think it is time for Nellie to put in her true cents . . . I mean her *two sense* . . . wait a second . . . *Je suis* . . . confused. Everything is happening in slow-motion. I. Mean. Every. Thing. Has. Completely. Slowed. Down.

Perhaps that is because I am not Nellie (per se). . . .

I am Nellie's *brain*.

"What?" you might be asking yourself. "How can that be?"

Well, technically, I am not her entire brain, either—just *une région*. The part that has not gone missing. The part that has not been rendered immediately and deeply unconscious. Obviously you will need to take my word on this since the way I work is a bit of a mystery. A conundrum, in fact.

As the world-renowned Brain Surgeon Roger Sperry once remarked, "In the human head there are forces within forces within forces, as in no other cubic half-foot of the universe...."

A Neurosurgeon observes hundreds of brains, up close and personal, so he should know.

Suffice it to say, I will be standing in for her until "Nellie" comes back. That is, *if* she comes back, which I sincerely hope she does, because without her we cannot possibly have any fun.

Now, if you would allow me a momentary indulgence, I will attempt to describe myself to you. Picture an organ weighing slightly over two pounds that floats inside your head. My surface is a maze of wormy gray ridges. I have a consistency that is gelatinous and wobbly, like Jell-O.

Mushy, thick, *pinkish gray* Jell-O, if you will.

My curious appearance gives few clues to how I operate. A common misconception is that I am strong and durable, yet I am actually quite delicate and easily bruised. For instance, if you should by chance have the unique opportunity to poke me with your little finger, I might *bleed*! This is why nature intended for me to be housed within your rock-hard skull. *N'est-ce pas?*

Between me and your skull are three protective membranes (the meninges), and surrounding those is a layer of watery fluid (the cerebrospinal fluid, or CSF), which acts like a cushion during movement, much like an airbag.

And speaking of airbags. When the car hit the tree, Nellie's body was thrown violently into the dashboard of the car. It was not my fault. I blame my immature, risk-taking prefrontal cortex for our injury, who not only thought it was a brilliant idea to drink those shots in the first place—but also to take off her seat belt.

Très irresponsable!

Thud. Bang. Glass shattered as the windshield imploded.

Nellie's forehead was slammed by the impact. Then, a split second later, I followed. Much like Jell-O in a bowl—should you drop or shake it—it takes a while for it to stop moving. That was me. Back and forth and back. Then twist.

Smashing right into her skull.

Shaken and outraged by the mere force of the accident and sensing the implications, I tried to find purchase. But it was quite difficult, as circuits started jamming, and parts of me began shutting down rather quickly, putting us into self-preservation mode. One two three . . . lights out.

Except not completely out because then we would be dead.

And obviously we are not. Not yet.

Nellie's side of the car was so badly crushed that the EMTs had to use the Jaws of Life—several types of hydraulic tools, known as cutters, spreaders, and rams—to cut her out.

wWrrrr, wWrrrrr.

Hang on. Hang on.

Then they hooked her up to life support for that perilous ride to the hospital. I must say, the sirens blaring and the ambulance racing down the highway were thoroughly unnerving in our precarious condition. But there was hope riding along with us: a Woman with cold fingers who was caressing Nellie's hand.

A few more minutes, sweetie, we're almost there.

The ambulance screeched up to the emergency entrance. Doctors shouted orders. *Stat. Stat.* We were wheeled down the corridor. *Go. Go. Go. Go.* And there were bright lights in the Emergency Room—I could sense them, even with Nellie's eyes closed.

In case you have not figured this out yet, Nellie is in a coma.

Coma by definition is not sleep (or amnesia) but an altered state of consciousness—one which the victim rarely remembers. In fact, what victims *do* remember depends on many factors, not the least of which is "where" the memory was stored. For example, upon "awakening," our girl might recognize all the letters of the alphabet but might not remember how to twirl spaghetti around a fork or brush her teeth—or how to do a double twist dismount off the balance beam.

But more on that later. . . .

"Coma happens" when there is serious brain injury. *Traumatic* brain injury—better known by the three-letter acronym TBI.

Once we left the Emergency Room, we were stabilized at Shock Trauma, where the Nurses put Nellie on a ventilator, or "vent." This basically means that they shoved a tube down her throat in order to expand her lungs with forced air so she could breathe.

At this very moment the machine is breathing for her, which, frankly, is one less thing for *me* to worry about. However, the presence of that tube makes her unable to expel mucus or anything else that could get lodged in her lungs. Fortunately they have another device they use, called a suctioning machine, just in case. The Doctor said, *She'll need a bit of suctioning now and then.*

Pas joli. Not pretty at all.

The other scary thing that can happen after a TBI is that the brain (or *moi*) may begin to swell. You have noticed that with other injuries, correct? Twisted ankles. Fractured fingers. The good thing about swelling is . . .

Merde! There are **no good things** about *brain* swelling, you imbecile!

The pressure could build up so intensely that I might not be able to stand it. And ironically, if I begin to swell within the confines of the skull, there is *nowhere else* for me to go. Despite my better judgment, I could begin to squeeze into a place I should not (like down into the brain stem), which could cause even more damage than the accident did in the first place.

In fact, Doctor is so worried about swelling that just a few minutes ago she drilled a hole into Nellie's skull and inserted an intracranial pressure monitor (ICP), which is an actual, three-inch metal bolt sticking out of Nellie's forehead. This is to relieve the pressure and make sure I behave myself.

Behave? Sadly, I do not have much of a choice.

Gratefully, in the last hour or two, things have begun to calm down. I am settling in. And there is much to learn about our new environment.

These are the interesting sounds of the Trauma Unit: Monitors beeping. Feet shuffling. Suctioning sounds, breathing sounds, hushed, low, and nursing sounds. *Not so good. No? Okay, put that tube there.*

Then other, more discrete noises filter in, gleaning me valuable information, since, as I said before, Nellie's eyes are closed.

I listen carefully. What was that? A familiar voice, a Woman's voice: terrified, panicked, confused. It is the muffled cry of Nellie's Mother! She is standing very near to us.

What do you mean coma? *Jim, what do they mean!?*

And then Father's halting sobs. *I don't know. This can't be happening!*

The intensity of worry, anguish, and disbelief coming from Nellie's Parents—it is overwhelming. I wish there were some way to comfort them. *She is going to make it,* I want to reassure them, *if I have anything to do with it!*

And of course, I do, my friends. *Absolument.* It **all** rests on me.

After a few minutes, another voice emerges. Dr. Franks enters the room. She introduces herself and says that the situation is very grave. Nellie has scored only a seven (out of a possible fifteen) on the GCS (Glasgow Coma Scale). She ticks items off a list: no eye opening, no verbal response, no motor response, et cetera.

You need to prepare yourselves, Mr. and Mrs. Perry. Your daughter has experienced severe head trauma. There's only so much we can do.

For some odd reason, I do not mind hearing this. In a sense, Dr. Franks is throwing down the gauntlet, issuing a challenge.

(How dearly I love a challenge—especially coming from a Brain Surgeon.)

Actually, I am quite confident that the Doctor has vastly underestimated my capabilities. What I want to say to her, but cannot, is simply this:

Frankly, Dr. Franks, no matter how far medical science has come, you will never completely understand me. No one is more motivated to get your patient better, because if Nellie does not survive . . . neither will I.

I need to stay focused. I must stay focused. We will **survive.** Uh, oh. What *is* that?

It is a sudden, dangerous shift in Nellie's blood pressure. Those dreadful machines have started beeping again. I find myself losing control.

We need to stabilize her, Mr. and Mrs. Perry. Please go. Now!

Alors, how much of this, you may wonder, does our sweet Nellie comprehend? Not much. You see, our girl has entered that liminal place where coma victims dwell: unconscious but not dead.

Breathing but not fully alive.

IS IT HOT HERE, SID? HELL, YEAH, IT'S HOT. WHO CAN SLEEP?
THE AVERAGE TEMPERATURE IS 126 DEGREES. . . .
—*Trey*

SID

I'm unconscious and dreaming a crazy dream. There's this big stage, at the *American Idol* tryouts, and I'm on it. My voice soars through the air, banging past the judges into the audience to the very back of the amphitheater. I'm so good, in fact, that I just know *I'm going to Hollywood*, until I choke, forget the lyrics, and then, crap, I'm done. The last thing I remember is Simon's voice snorting, "That, my dear, was ghastly."

Did the dream's ending wake me, or was it the chirping of those dang birds in the maple tree? It doesn't matter, because when I open my eyes there's my brother Miles, barefoot, in his camouflage pajamas.

"Siddy? Can I sleep with you?"

"Get in," I say, still groggy. Do all six-year-olds have a sun-just-peeked-over-the-horizon alarm clock hardwired into their bodies? My brother's breath smells like sour milk, and he's all elbows and knees.

"Y'all better close your eyes," I tell him. "And lay still. It's

Saturday. Way too early to get up." Doesn't my grandmother always tell him this, too?

I'm now *wide awake*, but, sweet relief, my mouth has finally stopped throbbing. It's been two days since that big-knuckled dentist gouged out my wisdom teeth. Finally I don't feel like somebody sucker-punched me in the face—from the *inside*.

When my brother's breath becomes slow and regular (*not* asthmalike wheezing), I take my phone off the dresser, pull on my fluffy robe, and trudge down the hall to the living room. Shutting the curtains to block the sun, I lie down on the couch and flip on CNN.

Another roadside bomb with seven troop casualties overnight.

So sad. I listen carefully for the location. *Not* Tikrit, which is a relief. My boyfriend, Treyshawn, is stationed in Iraq. He shipped out last September, taking with him his skin the color of blackberries and strong, thick legs that would wrap around mine so tightly that I thought he'd never leave me.

But he did. Just like everyone else.

His whole family is proud but sick with worry—who wouldn't be? But Trey says he's lucky. He believes he's got a guardian angel watching over him. Like one time he got hit by a taxi in Providence but didn't get hurt in the least. Besides, he says his new bunkmate, Dion, will protect him from the enemy, even if the crap army equipment can't.

Here's a question for the news media: Why do they say "casualties" when there is *nothing* casual about it? Why do they say "troops" when they really mean fathers and brothers and husbands and daughters and boyfriends?

Warphorisms. That was the name of a poem my friend Adam wrote in creative writing, which completely blew me away. There was this line about how war + euphemisms are like Maalox for the great American public, who like to digest their news between *Oprah* and *Jeopardy*. Isn't that so deep?

Anyway, I've sort of promised myself to Trey—even though he's almost twenty, which Grams thinks is way too old. Fingers crossed here, I'm hoping we'll get married someday. I know it might sound corny, but he's my soulmate. Trey says I shouldn't wait for him, but I want to. After all, he's sacrificing for our country. God bless our troops!

Around nine-thirty last night, my grandmother, who's a nurse at the VA hospital, called from work to check on me. *Phone turned off right now, girl. Your body needs to recuperate. Love you.* "Love you, too, Grams."

She was right. I *was* kind of tired, so I made an exception and shut off my phone and went to bed. Which is why it's kind of surprising to see all those new texts waiting for me this morning: twenty-two, to be exact.

The first is from Treyshawn. *Hurt much? If I was there I could make your mouth feel better—know what I mean?*

Isn't he sweet? There he is, living in a huge tent with Dion and three hundred other soldiers, and he still finds time to worry about me. I hug the phone to my chest. I miss him so much. Only a few more months till he comes home!

The next message is from Meredith, which is another surprise because she hardly ever texts me, because we kind of despise each other, because she is very two-faced and mean.

After I read it, though, my mouth drops open into a

perfect **O**. As in **oh**, my, gosh. Like she was texting so fast—it's only partly there.

Accident. Claire. Coma. Nellie?
Call me! NOW!!

I hurry to scroll through the rest of my messages, from Sara and Julia and Marissa—the news must have spread like wildfire. Everyone but me seems to know about this horrible car accident involving my best friend and her sister. I keep scrolling, but I can't seem to find the text that says,

whew, sorry, my b, they're going to be just fine.

Adam's message (from three in the morning) is the worst:

Sid? it was my fault.

What? Why?

I text him back right away, but he doesn't answer so I send another—telling him to call me IMMEDIATELY. The instant he wakes up.

Next, I'm running down the hallway as fast as I can, stumbling into my bedroom, throwing on any clothes from the floor, not caring if I wake Miles, but when he asks, *Where you going, Siddy?* I tell him my friends are in trouble, and I'm going to the hospital so I need to get dressed, which is hard without putting on the light, so could he please be quiet and go back to sleep?

Then, I bolt out of the room, almost crashing into my poor grandmother, who's standing outside my door. "Oops. Sorry, Grams."

"It's okay, Sid." A nest of fuzzy brown dreads spills over the front of her nightgown. She yawns and scratches the small birthmark on her face. "Thought I heard something. It's so early. What're you doing up?"

I can hardly get out the words. "S-something *terrible* has happened, Grams."

"What's the matter? Your brother's not sick?" She peers into his room. "Where is he, Sid?"

It makes sense she would worry about Miles. When he was little, after my father got fired, went bankrupt, and moved to Florida, my brother had to go to the ER lots of times and then to all of these breathing specialists because of his asthma attacks. It was very expensive. And scary.

"It's not Miles," I reply quickly. "He's asleep in my bed."

"What's wrong then? Not your mom?"

"No." But just last month my mother did run away from the group home again. They called us in the middle of the night to say she had gone missing, which happens sometimes when she refuses to take her pills. Luckily the next morning they found her, near the Pawtucket Bridge, carrying a pillowcase filled with cans of tuna fish.

"Would you just listen, Grams? It's not Miles or Mom. It's Claire and Nellie. They were in a really bad car accident last night!"

My grandmother leans against the wall, clutching the tiny silver cross she wears around her neck. "Oh, Lord, I'm so sorry. How awful. Tell me what happened, Sid. Please."

After we go sit on the couch in the living room, I tell her everything I know so far (which isn't much). Actually, I'm lying down, and my grandmother is massaging my feet in that relaxing way she's so good at. After I'm through, Grams convinces me that I can't go anywhere or call anyone yet 'cause no one is awake this early—except for Trey, I remind her, since it's already the middle of the afternoon in Tikrit.

"But I could call the hospital, right?"

"Of course." She hesitates. "They might not tell you much."

"I don't care. I need to do something!"

When I call the hospital, the lady says no visitors except family because Nellie's in critical condition.

"But what about Claire? Can't I go visit her?"

"She's due to be discharged later this morning."

I let out a sigh of semirelief, say thanks, and hang up—with so many unanswered questions swirling around in my mind.

What does it feel like to crash into a tree? That's what it said on the Channel Five News just now. The car looked destroyed. And the police are investigating "allegations" of a drinking party before the crash.

All of a sudden, I'm scared. I'm shivering I'm so scared.

I also feel guilty. Responsible. I should've tried to go to that party last night—no matter how much my teeth hurt. Ever since stupid Nick arrived on the scene last fall, Claire has been known to overindulge. This can't be happening to us!

It feels like somebody has poked a hole in my bubble of reality—I can almost hear it go *pop*. Because, I mean, these things are supposed to happen to other kids in other towns, somewhere else, *not here* in Blair's Cove. Especially not to me or any of my friends. Because, here's the thing: if *anything* can happen, *anywhere*, then maybe those guardian angels Trey believes in don't truly exist. And if that's the case, then I've got to start worrying for real.

I know he might not read it for days, but I jump on my computer and start on an e-mail to my boyfriend. I'm so upset that I end up typing the same exact message, all the way down the page:

r u okay? r u okay? r u okay?
r u okay? r u okay? r u okay?
r u okay? r u okay? r u okay?
r u okay? r u okay? r u okay?
r u okay? r u okay? r u okay?
r u okay? r u okay? r u okay?
r u okay? r u okay? r u okay?
r u okay? r u okay? r u okay?
r u okay? r u okay? r u okay?
r u okay? r u okay? r u okay?
r u okay? r u okay? r u okay?

But I don't press "send" because I don't want him to know how worried I am.

NO FISH WEARS A WRISTWATCH.
—*Making a Living Alongshore*

ADAM

"**M**an, what died in here?" Cookie says, pretend-coughing as he opens the passenger door to my Maxima. He's a big Asian kid with a crop of freckles on his sunburned legs. His real name is Jonathan Cookson, but nobody calls him that. He nods toward the ashtray. "Smoking again, I see?"

"Yeah, well," I admit. "They help me relax."

"Oh, man. You look *real* relaxed."

To be honest, I haven't been able to sleep or relax all weekend, worrying about Nellie in a coma, which is at the top of this huge pile of things I'm not relaxed about, including what will happen if/when Nick finds out that I told.

Usually I'm a closet smoker, because of the grief I get from my friends. I promise Cookie I'll quit when this is over. He ignores me and tosses the smoldering butt out the window.

"Um . . . I was working on that," I say weakly.

It bounces onto the curb of his driveway as I hang a right and head for school.

"Too bad," he replies. "I got your message from Friday

night, dude. Were you really in jail? I kept trying to text you back. What happened?"

"Pop confiscated my phone. I'm grounded for life. And there's this little matter of federal charges pending against me. Haven't you seen the news?"

"Yeah." Cookie takes a sip from his minicarton of orange juice. "Sorry. That sucks so bad. Nellie's still at the hospital, right? How's Claire holding up?"

"Like I said, I'm out of it. I have no clue." I hate being cut off from everyone, especially at a time like this. I ask him what rumors he's heard.

"Well, apparently Nick is going ape-shit. The cops brought him in for questioning over the weekend. They want to charge him as an adult, 'cause he's eighteen. He denied everything, of course. Wants to know who ratted him out. Said something all gangster, like, "When I find out who did this—heads will roll.""

I fumble around for another cigarette as Cookie tries to come up with theories about who the soon-to-be headless person might be. Usually this is the kind of banter we live for. Not today, I'm not in the mood. Obviously.

"*Moving on*," I say pointedly and give him a look.

When he finally gets it, he starts coughing on his drink. Orange juice actually shoots out his nose. "No. You didn't. You're shitting me, right?"

"Wish I was, my friend." I shake my head sadly. "Wish I was."

As I walk down the hallway, I notice that certain kids are giving me death stares or avoiding me altogether. It's mostly seniors who are doing this, Nick's cohorts, but Nellie's friends are acting awkward, too. Gossip seems to be the order of the day. For example, everyone seems to know that Claire's not at school, and that there will be some kind of assembly instead of first period. Cookie's homeroom is next to mine—he'll catch me at the assembly.

During homeroom, over the loudspeaker, Mr. Martin, our V.P., announces that guidance counselors will be available for anyone who's having a hard time dealing with the accident. "Kids who might be falling apart." He doesn't use those words exactly, but there are countless clichés to describe how I'm feeling: unglued, unhinged, falling apart. I hope Guidance has some kind of psychological duct tape to patch us back together again. Not likely.

They redid our auditorium last year, with new light and sound systems, and long, dark gray velvet curtains bracket the stage. After the juniors and seniors have piled in, they begin showing us that movie again, the one we saw in the beginning of the year. It's this boring, old movie (like from the eighties) about not drinking and driving—they feel obligated to do something, I guess.

When it's over and the credits start rolling, some of us move to stand up. But Mr. Martin, in his authoritative suit and tie, tells everyone to get back in their seats. Next, he introduces this middle-aged lady who's come in to talk to us. Her son was involved in a horrible, fatal, drunk-driving accident when he was only seventeen. He's been in prison for the past five years.

Aaaggh. Cookie gives me a look. My whole body feels numb.

"Most people focus on what happens to the victim," she says. "And while of course that is incredibly painful, I want to tell you about the other side."

There's barely a murmur as she describes how her son was driving home from a house party when he went the wrong way down a one-way street with his lights off and killed a girl who was walking her dog. He was arrested and spent two long years in home confinement, waiting for his trial. After which they threw him directly in jail.

"He only gets to make one phone call a week. For exactly ten minutes. We have to go through a metal detector to see him. And when we visit, we sit at those picnic tables with dozens of other families. He missed graduation. Going to college. Dating girls. He has no privacy there. None. He's spent the best years of his life rotting in a four-by-four cell."

I'm really glad Claire isn't around to hear this. I can barely take it myself.

Somebody raises their hand and asks what her son was like before the accident, if he ever got into trouble before.

"Not really. He was a good kid. Just like you kids. But unlike you, he made one mistake. Actually, he made several. My son refused a breathalyzer. He wouldn't say whose party he was at—or where they got the booze. The D.A.'s office doesn't take kindly to that. Oh, but he was, quote, 'protecting his friends.' I want to know where all his friends are now."

Mr. Martin looks at her sympathetically, then he thanks the lady for coming on such short notice. He repeats that the administration will do anything to prevent another tragedy from occurring again.

The room is getting warm. Mr. Martin adjusts his tie.

"One last thing. I know a few of you were at the police station over the weekend. We're not pleased—and Chief Rogers isn't happy with the 'lack of cooperation' from our students. But one of your peers did do the right thing. So, we'll be calling some of you down to the office this morning. And if anyone else knows something you're not telling us . . . ," Mr. Martin warns ominously. "We're determined to get to the bottom of this."

A few rows ahead of us, Nick is sitting with his usual group of thugs, including R.J. and this kid Jeff Chambers. After Mr. Martin steps away from the microphone, Nick turns around in his seat and points at me.

Then Nick makes like he's got a fake knife, pulls it across his throat, and mouths the words, "You're dead, man. So dead."

"Did you see that?" Cookie elbows me in the ribs.

I nod. "How much time do you think I have left?" I ask sarcastically.

Cookie smiles. "Hey, don't take this the wrong way, man, but I was wondering. You know your vintage Bob Marley T-shirt? The one with the sun in the background? It's always been my favorite."

I know he's joking, ha-ha, but I groan anyway, and my heart sinks.

We both know I can't wear it without a head.

THE SPOTTER WHO DOESN'T SPOT "ONCE" TO PROVE TO
THE GYMNAST THAT SHE IS READY TO BE ON HER OWN,
DESTROYS ALL TRUST PREVIOUSLY ESTABLISHED.
—*Gymnastics for Girls and Women*

CLAIRE

Thursday morning. It seems like I just fell asleep when my alarm clock starts buzzing: *get up, get up, get up.* Something pulls at my scalp: it's our yellow cat, Sandy, wanting to be fed. In the distance, there's the low rumble of thunder, and I can almost feel content (in a rain-pattering-against-the-windows sort of way). But then the images come crashing in.

It's like watching a DVD on fast-forward—except this is one movie you'd never want to see.

1. Headlights. Out of control. Hitting the tree.

2. Oxygen mask strapped onto my face.

3. My parents' faces, sick with fear, as they hurried into the ER.

4. Sitting on a metal gurney while the doctor finished taping my shoulder.

5. The worst scene of all: pressing my forehead against the cool glass wall of the Trauma Unit, thinking that person in there couldn't possibly be my sister. That wasn't her face all bloody and swollen, not her hands wrapped in gauze, not her leg stuck in a cast by her side. Tubes. Wires. Life support.

NO! Oh, my god. What have I done?

That was five days ago. The clock on my dresser says 6:45. Damn, I'm already late! I take a quick shower, hurrying, hurrying, and tug on my jeans just as Sid's grandmother, Pearl, pulls into our driveway and beeps the horn. *One second.* I wave from my window and hold up a finger. *Could you wait?* I have to feed Sandy.

The kitchen is quiet when I get downstairs. A bunch of dirty dishes sits in the sink, a stack of mail on the counter. There is no fresh coffee brewing, no scrambled eggs in a pan. My parents have slept at the hospital—*again*.

We haven't really had the chance to talk alone because our relatives have been around constantly for support. It feels so surreal. Uncle Ray and Aunt Lucy have taken turns bringing me to the hospital, or I've been home on my own. Whenever my parents drop in—to grab a quick shower or to check on me—their faces are gaunt, eyes hollow as ghosts, and they don't stay for very long.

The horn beeps again from Pearl's blue van. I choke down a stale Nutri-Grain bar, grab a bottle of water, and lock the door behind me. Outside, the light drizzle of rain makes the hair on my arms stand on end. I'm halfway down the front walk when I realize I've forgotten my keys . . . and my backpack . . . and to feed Sandy.

Frigging fantastic! My head is screaming.

Sid lowers the car window. We've been best friends since fourth grade when she moved here to live with Pearl. Most of the time we don't even have to finish each other's sentences. "What's wrong?" she asks.

(She means besides the obvious.)

"I forgot my backpack. To feed our cat. I'm locked out."

Pearl points to the garage door, which someone—Mom? Dad? me?—left open all night. The door into the house from the garage is unlocked, so I can get in that way, but it creeps me out just the same. Some psycho-stranger could have come in last night and murdered me in my sleep.

Not that I don't deserve it.

Running up the stairs to my room, I keep repeating *backpack, keys, feed Sandy.* I seem to have trouble remembering the simplest things. Dr. Franks said I might experience some confusion over the next few days, but that my shoulder should be fine. *There's no reason Claire can't go back to school.*

Of course, she doesn't have to face everyone like I do.

I try to hurry, but when I get eye-to-eye with a photograph framed on the wall over my desk, I freeze. The picture was taken about six years ago, after we'd won our very first team championship. Nellie is doing a split in the center front row, holding our trophy high over her head. Sid is there with her hair in cornrows, and Julia's still in braces. Lindsey, Katie, and Marissa, all of us posed in our team jackets, red and white.

We're all happy, smiling, *normal.* The pressure of a sob forms at the back of my throat. *Don't think about it. Don't think about it. Don't think.*

My backpack is under my bed.

Keys, feed Sandy. Keys, feed Sandy.

Down the stairs, two at a time. Kitty chow into the bowl. Keys from under the stack of mail. This time I go out through the garage door.

"Any news since yesterday?" Pearl asks as I slide into the backseat next to Miles. The radio is turned to a morning talk show.

"Mom called to say goodnight. Nellie still isn't responding."

Sid turns around. "They still don't know when she's going to come out of it?"

Don't say *if*. Don't say *if*.

But my mind says it anyway.

"Right. It could take a while. That's why I'm going back to school."

Pearl puts the van in reverse and pulls out of the driveway. Funny, even if my life has been shattered, our house doesn't look any different: it's still a white raised ranch with the trampoline in the side yard, Mom's window boxes planted with bright red geraniums, and Nellie's bedroom on the second floor (next to mine) with the lace curtains.

When Pearl turns onto Waterview Road, a school bus stops for some little kids on the corner. Pearl waits, then we drive past the marshes and the sandy beach, where Sid and I used to go swimming in the summertime. Unexpectedly, my stomach growls loudly, and Miles offers me his nearly empty container of Cheerios. "No thanks. I'm not hungry."

Pearl glances back. "You're taking care of yourself, Claire?"

"No . . . I mean . . . yes, I ate at home."

Pearl smiles in the rearview. "You know, one of our boys at the VA came home with a head injury. They thought he wasn't going to make it, but he's doing fine now. And he was comatose, just like Nellie."

"What's wrong with Nellie's toes?" chirps Miles. "I thought it was just her brain that could be dead."

"*Miles!*" Sid turns around again, hoop earrings swinging. "Sorry, Claire."

Pearl catches my eye. "Little ones have a hard time understanding."

I try to put on a brave smile. "It's okay. I mean, Miles is right. There's a chance she might not get any better."

"Don't even *think* that!" Sid says. "She's got to, right?"

After that, it gets awkward in the car. And I can't help but wonder if we're all thinking the same thing. What if my sister doesn't get better? Then what?

And they don't even know the worst part yet. Nobody does. I haven't told anyone . . . not my parents, not the police . . . not even Sid.

Because if I have to admit to anyone how I felt right before I tried to pass Adam's car—well, I just don't think I can deal.

I mean, how do you live with the fact that you were the one who caused this devastating thing to happen to your own sister? That for a split second, maybe you wanted something bad to happen to her? Not the worst thing—you didn't want that. But what if part of you secretly wished that she wouldn't be so annoying anymore, so perfect, the favorite, the *best*? What if you didn't even know that you were wishing it . . . until it happened?

What would you do if your wish . . . your horrible wish . . . came true?

NELLIE'S BRAIN

It is time for lunch. Here comes Slacker Nurse . . . again. I can tell by her smell: the cheap odor of fast food lingers on her clothing.

I do not like this one. Not one bit. It seems to take her forever to attach the feeding tube to the hole in our stomach. And she refuses to keep Nellie's body upright for the standard thirty to forty-five minutes recommended after our feeding.

Bumbling idiot!

Incroyable. We are at her mercy as long as Nellie stays in this coma.

At least the Nice Nurse rearranges Nellie's arms and legs every few hours so she will not develop those grotesque bedsores—or contracture. This is when muscles atrophy permanently because they are not being worked in the usual way. Actually, all the Aides and Therapists do this, except for this one: Slacker. She has not once adjusted Nellie's position since her shift began.

Progress update: Our girl has been posturing since yesterday. *Qu'est-ce que c'est* posturing?

Basically this means that her limbs are flexing inward

72

toward her body, which increases her points on the Glascow Coma Scale. The doctors consider this promising. But every time she postures, the fluid around her brain (ahem, *moi)* increases to dangerous levels, which, as I have said before, is bad, very bad.

That is why the Nurses are monitoring her carefully—or at least most of them are. If I could only communicate this to the powers that be: *Frankly, Dr. Franks, I am more than a bit apprehensive when Slacker is in charge!*

But unfortunately, I cannot communicate anything at the moment. All I can do is passively wait as our body takes its nourishment from a plastic packet.

Tell me the truth, is it hot in here? Rehab was an hour ago, but I still feel warm. They began rehabbing Nellie five days ago, soon after we arrived at Shock Trauma. To be perfectly honest, it is exhausting.

Smell this. Can you feel that? Was that an eyelid flutter?

Rehab is wearing me out. All I want to do is rest without somebody yelling in Nellie's ear every five minutes: *Squeeze my hand, Nellie. If you can hear me, squeeze my hand.*

Is it necessary for her recovery? *Mais oui!* Of course it is! But obviously, if I could make her hand squeeze, I would. Nothing would give me greater pleasure. **I am trying my best here, people!**

"All done here?" asks Slacker, as if we could reply.

Apparently the last remains of our bland nutrients have dripped down from the tube. She wheels it away. Next, a motor whirs, and *quelle surprise!* Once again, Slacker is putting us flat on our back much too soon. *Bleh.* Our stomach feels full and bloaty.

Double Bleh!

What else have we been up to, besides posturing and rehabbing and feeding, you might ask? When there are not any crises, it is quiet in Shock Trauma. Visitors are limited to immediate family. Nellie's Parents were here, and now they have gone down to the café for a snack. Let us hope they will enjoy it more than we did.

In our room the television drones, some tiresome reality show. It is interesting that they have assigned one to us (not a reality show, but a TV) since neither Nellie nor her Roommate (whose name is Gina) is able to watch it. Wishful thinking, perhaps?

Yes, television is for the Visitors, I suppose, although I have caught Slacker watching it when she is not blathering on her mobile telephone. That is what she is doing right now, secretly in the bathroom. *Nellie's* bathroom. Can they not afford a bathroom for Staff?

These are the trivial matters which occupy my day.

As you can see, time passes slowly when you are recovering from a traumatic brain injury. There is not much to do, except to spy on the incompetents and to think. But I like thinking, *n'est-ce pas?* Especially in French.

It was during our recent trip to Paris that Nellie developed an affinity for the language of romance. On scheduled breaks from the competition, she loved to stroll with the other Gymnasts, along the banks of the murky Seine. I believe this is when all of those pretty-sounding words were seared indelibly into our memory, along with useful foreign phrases. *Vive la France!*

But, oddly enough, musing about our lovely excursion (when we were happy, mobile, and free) makes me feel depressed all of a sudden. Not only does it depress me, but it confuses me as well. *Mais oui,* I am feeling suddenly quite depressed and disturbed and confused and disoriented and **hot.**

Yes, it actually *is* hot in here. Not my imagination. *Il fait chaud.*

Hello? Where is Slacker?

She really needs to turn down the temperature or open a window, because it is stuffy and claustrophobic—as if we are not getting enough air.

Breathe in. Breathe out.

Uh, oh. Now those infernal monitors are beeping again, which means that Nellie's heart rate is up, and her blood pressure. *Mon dieu!* There is a burning in her throat. Somebody better do something—fast!

Merde.

Too late. More evidence that things have spun completely out of my control. On the front of Nellie's hospital gown, I register a wet, clammy sensation.

The bathroom door squeaks open. I can sense someone standing at the foot of the bed. "Oh, damn, girl. What did you do?"

What did *we* do?

The pungent smell of vomit fills the room.

An intercom button crackles. "Hello?" says Slacker. "I'm in room 302. Can someone get down here? Like now?"

I hear the patter of rubber-soled shoes in the hall. Nice Nurse rushes into the room. "Don't just stand there!" she shouts. "Get some paper towels. What happened? Did you put her head down too fast after that last feeding?"

"Of course not!"

LIAR!

Nice Nurse touches Nellie's forehead. "My goodness, she's burning up. I think she's aspirating. Quick! Get the oxygen and the suction machine while I turn her over on her side. And call Dr. Franks to order some antibiotics. *Stat.* Where's her family?"

Slacker pauses. "In the cafeteria, I think."

"Okay. Well, let's clean up this mess—then page them. Poor little cupcake, it'll be a miracle if she makes it."

WHAT WE GET TO EAT? THEY'RE CALLED MRES. THAT MEANS
MEALS READY TO EAT—STUFF SMELLS NASTY. BUT SOMETIMES
GOOD THINGS HAPPEN. LIKE YESTERDAY, WHEN ME AND
DION WERE TRANSPORTING FOOD TO THIS TOWN THAT DIDN'T
HAVE ANY? THESE LITTLE KIDS WERE ALL SMILES, LIKE WE
WERE SOME KIND OF DAMN SANTA CLAUS. DAYS LIKE THAT,
THEY'RE RARE, SID. BUT WHEN THEY DO HAPPEN? IT ALMOST
FEELS LIKE WE'RE S'POSED TO BE HERE.
—*Trey*

SID

Like swarms of black flies in the summertime, everyone
comes buzzing at us as soon as we walk into the cafeteria.
Claire says it's been like this all morning. "Is your sister okay?"
"She's still in a coma, right?" "When's she coming home?"

Two kids from ninth grade nervously approach us. "Is it
true Nellie will never be able to walk again?"

Claire practically bites off their heads. "No, that's not true
at all. So mind your own business, okay?!"

I had to ask them to give us some space.

Truth be told, I assumed it was going to be crazy with drama
on Claire's first day back to school—but not this crazy. We are
standing in line for today's special: seafood tacos. When Claire
looks back at me, I notice her lips have turned that pasty color
they sometimes get right before competitions.

As we walk toward our usual lunch table, Adam is already

sitting there with his tray. After three days of suspension, he's back at school, too. It's the first time I've seen him since the accident—Grams let me stay home on Monday to be with Claire. Cookie told me on Tuesday that Adam was suspended. And, poor Adam, his dad took away his phone, too. I have to say, he looks kind of grim.

"Hey, Sid," he calls. "Claire?"

But Claire doesn't see him, or she's choosing to ignore him, because that girl just keeps right on walking past.

"Can we just sit by ourselves today?" she says to me. "Please?"

"Later," I say to Fish, shrugging as his sad eyes meet mine. He and I have fourth period together today. So later means before chorus, my favorite class, and right after lunch.

I ask a teacher if we can take our trays out into the hallway, and she says yes automatically, because everyone knows what my friend has been through.

Leaning against the wall, I bite into my taco, which despite the wilted lettuce isn't bad.

Claire absently picks at her salad. "Did you hear that R.J. was locked up yesterday?" she asks. "He used a fake ID to buy the kegs. The judge wanted to teach him a lesson. And Nick is suspended for two more days. He might have charges pressed against him, too."

I heard about her loser boyfriend—or is it *ex*-boyfriend?— and all those kids from the party being suspended after the assembly on Monday, along with Adam. A lot of us had started posting get-well messages for Nellie on her Facebook page, but then a few people started trashing Fish on it, saying he was the narc, so that's how it got all over school.

"Don't forget about Adam," I say. "He's in trouble, too. Did they get the beer in Massachusetts or something? Somebody said he was transporting across state lines."

Claire shrugs. "Well, he should've thought about that . . . *before*. Admitting what he did is one thing, Sid. But why did he have to rat out everyone else? Now I have to go to court, too. They want to charge me with reckless driving. And driving under the influence, which isn't true! My blood test will come out fine, but I'm so scared."

I don't know what to say to this. When I look at her again, she's almost in tears. "Maybe it was too soon for me to come back to school, Sid. All those questions. I can hardly breathe."

Her whole body is trembling as I give her a hug. "They're just worried about you. Everyone's worried. They don't know how to show it, is all."

She's acting like she's not convinced. "Are you serious? Haven't you heard what they're saying in the hallways? In the lunchroom? Everybody blames me, I can tell."

Why is she being so paranoid?

"Nobody blames you. It was an accident, right? Everyone knows that."

"Do *you*?" she asks. Even though she's told me next to nothing, she should know that I would never blame her—no matter what.

So, I repeat, "Of course," but here's the thing: If she wasn't drinking, I don't understand why she tried to pass Fish's car that night. Like maybe she's leaving out some of the details? Besides, we've driven on that road together hundreds of times. She knows how crazy it would be to pass.

"Listen, Claire, I sort of get why they might be confused. Maybe it would help if you break it down for them. Like, why *did* you—"

All of a sudden, her eyes flash, a glimpse of green, like a horsefly before it bites. "Didn't you hear me?!" she explodes. Then I guess she must notice the look on my face. "Sorry. It's too hard, Sid. I can't talk about it yet. Please be my friend and don't ask, okay?"

Before I can stop her, she gets up and runs down the hall, leaving me with her tray—and more confused than I already was.

∽

After lunch, I go to creative writing and slip into the seat beside Adam. He's wearing a Dave Matthews T-shirt and gray cargo shorts, and his legs are stretched out in front of him. "Hey, Sid." He tries to smile, but his eyes stay sad.

Miss Appleton has put our assignment on the board. This week, we've been watching clips from *Saving Private Ryan*. She wants us to write a response poem to today's segment using metaphors.

Lovely. I can't write poetry for crap, and obviously war movies remind me too much of Trey. After we hand in yesterday's homework, Miss A. turns on the DVD. Blood. Bombs. Somebody's arm flying off—and that's only the first two minutes.

I lean over to Adam. "So, how are you doing? You didn't miss much these past few days."

"Hard to say."

I point at the fading bruise on his cheek leftover from his fight at the party. "Cookie said R.J. looked worse," I say quietly.

He doesn't return my smile. "Why didn't you guys sit with me in lunch today? Claire thinks I'm a narc, right? Like everybody else."

"No, she doesn't. She's just upset. I mean, wouldn't you be?"

Miss Appleton is dressed in a crisp white blouse and black skirt. She's usually easy to get off topic and doesn't mind if you talk with your voice low—but not today. From behind her desk, she puts a finger to her lips, "Shhhhh!" like we'd better shut up—or else.

"Yeah, of course," he whispers. "I'd be insane. I can't believe . . . I never meant . . . this is so crazy, Sid." Then his eyes get all watery, and he wipes his face with the back of his hand.

I watch as he takes out a pen and begins to scribble something in his binder. He's writing words like "courage," "hero," "pain."

Poor Adam. Suddenly, I get this urge to throw my arms around him and say: *Don't worry, we'll get through this. Nellie will come out of her coma—Trey will come home soon, and in a few months everything will be back to normal, okay?*

Hey, I want somebody to do that for *me*!

But the next thing I know, a teacher is at the door calling for Miss Appleton to come into the hallway. They talk for a few minutes, then Miss A. motions for me with her out-stretched hand.

"Sid? Could you come here, please? Quickly. Bring your things."

What? So unfair! Weren't other people talking, too?

"You need to report to Guidance, Sid. Hurry up," Miss Appleton says as I come into the hall.

I've never seen a teacher cry before. She holds a finger to her eye to keep the tears from running into her mascara.

"Guidance?" I ask. "What's wrong?"

"Nellie's not doing so well. Claire wants you to go with her. Her uncle is here to pick her up. She has to go to the hospital . . . to say . . . good-bye."

I DID MY BEST, IT WASN'T MUCH
I COULDN'T FEEL, SO I TRIED TO TOUCH
I'VE TOLD THE TRUTH, I DIDN'T COME TO FOOL YOU
AND EVEN THOUGH IT ALL WENT WRONG
I'LL STAND BEFORE THE LORD OF SONG
WITH NOTHING ON MY TONGUE BUT HALLELUJAH
—*Lyrics by Leonard Cohen*

CLAIRE

"It almost looks like she's sleeping," Sid whispers.

"Well, she's not," I reply, and I'm too stressed out to explain the difference. Or to tell her why Nellie's hands are in those big white cotton mittens which are shaped just like boxing gloves. "So she won't scratch herself," the nurse had explained. "Or bruise her hand on the bed rail. Or try to pull out her feeding tube."

This past week I've learned more about coma victims and hospitals and procedures—more than anyone I know, except maybe my parents.

I was a complete wreck the entire drive here. Sid kept trying to chatter away to my Uncle Ray about random things, clearly nervous, until she finally gave up and began humming, which is one thing about Sid, no matter how horrible the situation, she's always got a song in her head.

This is the second time my sister has "coded" since the accident. How much more can any of us take?

The hallway is busy with nurses in green scrubs and doctors with face masks, scurrying in and out. My parents are in ICU talking to Dr. Franks. I peer in again through the glass window.

Nellie's left eye is still closed, and purple, and swollen to the size of an Easter egg. Her neck is in a brace with a tube coming out of her throat—and she's plugged into even more machines than the other day. Red and green flashing lights, a computer monitor, and dozens of wires are coiled and twisted around one another like the overlapping tracks of a roller coaster ride.

Except this is one ride you'd never want to take.

I'm so scared. My mind keeps repeating the words too horrible to say aloud: *Please don't die. Please don't die. Please don't die.*

Nellie doesn't answer, of course. But for some reason it feels like I can hear her, through the glass, through the bandages, inside her head.

Where am I, Claire? Where are you? Why can't you help me get out?

Next to me, Sid is silently weeping; I feel her touch my hand. It's been raining all day. Outside, there is a loud crack of thunder, and the lights flicker.

"What if the electricity goes out?" I wonder aloud. "Those machines are the only things keeping my sister alive." Sid says they've got to have a backup system in place.

My father comes out of ICU first. "They've got her stabilized again. Thank god. Dr. Franks says we'll just have to wait and see."

I swallow hard. "So that means we don't have to say good-bye?"

He's instantly angry. "Do what you think is right, Claire." The muscles twitch on the side of his face.

Sid gently pats his arm. "But is it okay if we stay and visit her?"

"That's fine." He shakes his head wearily. "Prepare yourself. You're probably not going to get a response."

My mother comes out next. Her short auburn hair is matted down like someone who's spent the past week sleeping in a hospital chair. She looks so tired and small. "Oh, hello, Sid. How's your grandmother, honey? Thanks so much for coming by. I know this isn't easy."

"No, I *want* to be here," Sid replies. After they hug, Sid asks my mother if there's anything special we should do when we go into the room.

"Sometimes they respond to music—or familiar voices. That's what the nurses keep telling us. Encourage her, I guess. Be positive. Tell her that you believe in her."

"That's easy," says Sid, smiling. "I do believe in her. She'll be okay, Mrs. Perry. Nellie will pull through this. I just know she will."

I'm thinking it's easy for Sid to be positive. Sid wasn't at the party. Sid wasn't driving the car. I'd give anything to trade places with Sid right now (or with anyone else in the entire world). Even, I realize—no, *especially*—with Nellie.

When we go into the room, my sister is lying still, breathing through a respirator. All we can hear is the raspy sound of her breath and the steady *beep, beep, beep* of the machines. Sid goes up to "talk with her" while I sit near her feet and stare at her toes, which are sticking out from the bottom of the cast.

Reaching out gingerly, I touch them. They feel smooth and cool. And her toenails are polished the same glittery blue that she painted them the night of the party.

But her feet aren't moving. They are so vulnerably still. I've sat next to my sister's feet millions of times, watching her chalk them up. I've seen them soaring over the vault, flying through the air. One thing you could count on: her feet were always in motion.

"Move," I say, frustrated. "Damn it! Move your feet, Nellie. I know you can do this! Come on!"

But she doesn't move her feet . . . or her toes . . . or anything.

In the meantime, Sid is sitting at the head of the bed, holding Nellie's hand. She's quietly singing this song they sang for concert choir this past spring. Ever since Jason Castro performed it on *American Idol*, it's become one of Sid's favorites.

"Hal-le-lu-jah, Hal-le-lu-jah, Hal-le-lu-u-u-u-jah."

The song is so pretty and mournful, and Sid's voice is so clear, almost like an angel's, that I can't help it—before long, I'm staring at the floor with tears streaming down my face. Because what if it's the last song Nellie ever hears?

But suddenly Sid stops singing and gasps, "Oh, my lord, baby Jesus!"

I brace myself for the worst. Seriously, I'm about to run out of the room and get my parents when Sid smiles at me with the biggest smile on her face.

"Look, Claire, look at that!"

And I look. I can't believe it. Nellie has opened her eye!

"Yeah, girlfriend." Sid grins at me with her beautiful smile, dancing her shoulders back and forth. "And you know what? I'm pretty sure your sister just squeezed my hand!"

QUAHOGS ARE FOUND IN THE TOP 3 INCHES OF SANDY OR
SAND-AND-MUD BOTTOMS, USUALLY BELOW THE LOW-TIDE
LINE. IT'S EASIER TO DIG FOR THEM AT LOW TIDE.
—*Eleanor Ely*

ADAM

It's Saturday morning. Pop flicks on his turn signal for Main Street in Pascoag, which is lined with antique stores and tacky souvenir shops. He moors his boat at the Pascoag Marina, 'cause it has better access to the bay. He takes charters out from here, too. Although lately business hasn't been great.

When we get out on the bay, the water is choppy, with a stiff breeze creating white caps like out at sea. High puffs of gray clouds checker the sky. As the boat bumps along, I hang my arm overboard and trail my fingers in the foamy wake; we're heading out to the flats.

A half-hour later, we arrive in a small cove about ten yards off shore. This is one of Pop's favorite spots; a dry shoal, with just a couple of inches of water.

While my father slows and cuts the motor, I pull on my gators 'cause the water's cold and hop over the side. I prefer to rake from the water, 'cause it's easier, but Pop likes to dig from the boat using this heavy rake that has moving parts (and from a distance kind of looks like a huge salad tong).

After we both bring up a pile of clams, I climb back in

and sort them—cherrystones, chowders—and put them into red onion sacks according to size. Then I get back out and dig some more.

When we finally reach our quota, a "three barrel" day, my dad peers into the Styrofoam cooler and cracks open a can. I'm hot and thirsty, so I rummage around for a Gatorade.

The good thing about clamming is you're usually done by noon. But for some reason today my father seems glued to his flimsy green-and-white beach chair, clueless that I might need a shower or want to play Guitar Hero or do anything other than wait for him to finish his near-beer.

"Can we go now?"

"Sure." He scratches the stubble on his chin. "Sure, we can. But first I wanna ask you something. That's a bad road for kids to be passing on. Were you messing around with your car?"

Now? After a whole week, he's asking me about this *now*?

I snag a bag of chips from the cooler and begin scarfing them down.

He takes another swig. "I only ask because I heard something from the guys at the boathouse. Guess I should watch the news. I'm trying to figure out how good of a lawyer we need. Why didn't you tell me those girls were trying to pass your car?"

For the same reason I tell him as little as possible about my personal life: he just wouldn't understand. But obviously I've replayed it in my head a zillion times. *Was* I messing around? I didn't think so. I mean, the first time they tried to pass me I was still pissed about getting slammed by Nick. Nellie was yelling something, and I thought she was laughing at me, so yeah, I gave them the finger, ha-ha, like it was all a big joke, and then I sped up.

But that second time? Why *were* those girls even trying to pass me that second time?

My father clears his throat. "Well?"

"They were trying to pass me, Dad. I don't know why. I was ahead of them. A car was coming the other way. I guess they didn't have room to get back in."

"And so they went off the side of the road?"

"Yeah. I heard the crash behind me as they hit the tree. It was the worst sound ever," I explain, the words flowing now. "But I feel guilty as hell. Maybe I should have pulled over somehow. I can't stop thinking about it. I mean, Nellie is still in the hospital—"

My father jumps up. "Are you thinking it's your fault? Because it's not. I mean, we should get a lawyer, but it sounds like nothing you did *caused* the accident. You brought the keg. Admit to that. But don't say nothing to incriminate yourself at your hearing, okay? Hopefully they won't try and sue us."

"But if it wasn't for me, there wouldn't have even *been* a party."

He looks at me strangely. "That's crazy! Kids your age? They would've found a way to have that party—with or without you. Why are you thinking like that? That kind of thinking can get you in a shitload of trouble."

Was he completely naïve?

"In case you haven't noticed, Dad, I'm already in trouble. I could end up locked up—or with a permanent record 'cause of this. And everybody from that party hates me now. Even Claire. They all think I'm a freaking narc."

Pop shakes his head, mumbling, "Goddamn nitwit teenagers." Then he reaches over and picks up a sack of clams. With his right hand, he works one edge of his shucking knife into the tiny space between the shells.

Finally, he holds the clam out to me.

"Thanks. I'm good." I wave him off. He knows I hate them raw.

"Okay, but look." He points to the small, black siphon sticking out of the clam's body. "See that little neck right there? Did you know clams can filter over a gallon of water an hour? All the crap the sewers dump into the bay? It doesn't bother them a bit."

"*So?*" I think we learned that in like seventh grade.

"How do you think I get by? After everything I've been through?"

Oh, *sweet.* Now he's going to start on what a screwed up childhood he had—stories I've heard a thousand times before. But when Mom left us for her cactus-loving boyfriend, that's when his world completely blew apart. Correction: it blew apart after Molly. Funny, he never wants to talk about *that.*

"Adam, I asked you a question."

"What? I don't know, Pop. How do you deal?"

"Filters." My father holds the clam to his lips, slurps it down, and leans back in his chair, as if I'm supposed to know what the hell he's talking about.

"Filters. So obvious. Thanks. That explains everything."

He shakes his head. "What I mean is, you got to keep pushing through the bad shit," he says forcefully. "Or you won't ever get to the good on the other side. I'm proud you told the truth. Even if those kids are mad at you. We'll get through this. Nothing you did caused that accident. Forget about it. Don't waste time blaming yourself for things that ain't your fault—not like I've done my whole damn life."

"And what if I can't forget about it?"

"Okay, maybe you never will *forget* it. But you can *learn* from it. You're a strong kid, Adam. Stronger than me. Always have been. You gotta find yourself some good filters. Something positive to think about. And move on."

Smoky gray clouds begin to gather low at the horizon. He stands up again. "Looks like we're gonna get a little weather. Pull up the anchor, okay?"

After lighting a cigarette, he starts the motor, and we fight the current all the way in. By the time we pull into the snug harbor, I'm thinking maybe he's got a point. Maybe what happened to Nellie *wasn't* completely my fault. With a little luck, she might even be okay . . . *eventually.*

But I'm not sure I'll ever be able to forget that night. Or figure out what I'm supposed to learn from the images that continue to haunt me. Like the sound of that tree cracking. And the color of blood lit only by moonlight. Or Nick's fingers ready to slit my throat.

I LIKE NONSENSE; IT WAKES UP THE BRAIN CELLS.
—*Dr. Seuss*

NELLIE'S BRAIN

"That's it. Put your tongue on the roof of your mouth. Nel-lie. Nel-lie. Can you say your name?" This is what Speech Therapist is telling our girl to do. In the sunlight, a thin gold chain sparkles at the base of his throat.

"Nah Nah Nah," Nellie moans. She thrashes her arm—or was that her leg?

J'en ai assez! It is frustrating.

For some reason I am not able to help her utter a word that makes any sense, or properly control her appendages, or do anything even remotely like what we could do . . . *before.*

Progress update: one week + one day since the ACCIDENT.

Status: Nellie survived the "feeding-tube crisis." But as Doctor likes to remind us, the "re"turn to self after coma is not easy. Nor is it a straight path to recovery. Recovery can be a roller coaster of events and emotions for Patients and their Families.

Something positive did come out of that particular crisis, however: Slacker was transferred to another floor.

Good riddance!

Yet, despite the setbacks, at least our girl is making progress. Nellie is gradually becoming more aware of her surroundings. Her eyes are open more often than not. A pinprick on the bottom of her foot causes a flinch, a kick, or a yelp.

Also, Dr. Franks took Nellie off the vent last night. Therefore, she is breathing on her own again—or should I say that *I* am back in charge of her breathing? She is also talking— or to be more specific, she is *attempting* to talk.

This morning Speech Therapist is working with her, urging her onward. "Nel-lie. Nel-lie," he repeats. "Come on. You can do this."

"Na-na-na." She dissolves into tears.

Je suis désolé. I *am* trying.

It is almost ten o'clock on Sunday morning. People are gathering in the corridors. Visiting hours will begin soon. Unfortunately, some Patients—like Nellie's ex-Roommate, Gina, for example—do not get too many.

Gina is a fifteen-year-old who acquired her brain injury by falling (whilst inebriated) two stories from the balcony of the mall. Yesterday, the Healthcare Professionals were discussing Gina's imminent discharge with the Social Worker. And earlier this morning, she was sent to a "long-term care facility" because of her PVS.

Persistent. Vegetative. State.

This is the term nobody wants to hear. Not Families or Friends, or even the Staff who work here, who (I have since learned) tend to become quite attached. It is what coma Victims are labeled after a month—or up to a year—of nonresponding. PVS is so unspeakably sad that if I could access my emotional center, I would curse the brutal unfairness of it, the tragic waste of a young, healthy life!

And yet, *mes amis*, there is no point in dwelling on something that depressing. W*e* are decidedly *not* in that situation.

Nellie will **not** be going to a long-term care facility. She is emerging. She is now a Level 3 (out of 8) on the Rancho Los Amigos Scale, another measure of her progress, this time in a positive direction. Dr. Franks informed her Parents that she will soon be transferred to a state-of-the-art Rehabilitation Center near Boston. A reason to celebrate. *C'est merveilleux!* Strike up the band.

The murmuring in the corridor grows louder now. I imagine Nurses are busy in all of the rooms. Patient beds are motored into upright positions. Feeding tubes are removed. Bed pans whisked away. In fact, there are so many noises during visiting hours that it is sometimes difficult to parse out the important ones . . . what *is* that?

Speech Therapist asks, "Do you hear someone, Nellie?"

Familiar voices at the threshold to the room. And then, like a jolt of electricity, something changes. Circuits that were jammed before somehow twist free. Her head turns. Eyes open wide. She begins to focus; she is tracking.

Who is that? Someone she knows. Someone she loves.

It takes tremendous effort, but I help her to move the muscles in her face, her mouth, her tongue. Her heart skips a beat.

"Hi, Care."

To have too much hope leaves little room for grief.
To grieve too much swallows hope.
—*Listening in the Silence, Seeing in the Dark*

CLAIRE

"Did you hear that? Nellie just said my name!"
The speech therapist flips his chart closed and says,
"You're right. Good job, Nellie. That's all for today."

Mom can hardly contain herself. She rushes to my sister's
bedside. "That was great! Are you really back here with us?"

"Maaaa-maaaa?" Nellie slumps back onto the pillow, eyes
closed again, as if this small step has taken almost everything
out of her.

The nurse strides over and puts a hand on my mother's
shoulder. "We've turned another corner. Your daughter's been
more responsive for the past ten hours or so."

"Thanks so much, Grace. It's been the longest week of
our lives."

My father shakes his head. "That's for sure."

This particular nurse has short white hair cropped close to
her head, blue eyes, and tanned, leathery skin. She goes to the
foot of the bed to adjust the splints on Nellie's heels. They've
explained that the splints are supposed to make it less painful
when my sister begins walking again—but now she grimaces
in pain.

"Ahh. Ahh."

"Sorry," Grace says. "I know this hurts, dollface."

Those frigging splints—Nellie's feet aren't meant to be stuck in those things. "Do you have to make them so tight?" I say, protesting.

"I know. But it's good she can feel them now."

My mother sits on the edge of the chair, running her hand down Nellie's arm. "It's been so stressful waiting to see if . . ." She stops herself. "What should we do now? What should we say?"

"Dr. Franks would tell you to try to orient her," Grace replies. "Tell her where she is. What day it is."

What *day*?

My father's eyes dart over to mine. We both know that today is the Bay State Invitational, the meet where Nellie was supposed to qualify for Nationals in Florida. Last night, our coach, Melissa, had called to ask if (there were the slightest chance) I might compete today with the rest of the team—but I said no. Not today, next week—or maybe ever.

My sister seems to have fallen asleep again. The sun is too bright so Grace pulls the curtains half-closed.

My mother's face relaxes into a smile. "It's just such good news. Nellie's talking, I mean. Isn't it, Jim?"

Dad squints and cleans his eyeglasses. "Yes, I suppose it is."

"Well, it's certainly a step in the right direction," Grace says, placing a metal water pitcher on the tray table. "She'll be up and walking in no time."

"But what about gymnastics?" I ask, because if my sister *is* improving, I'm desperate to hear there's still hope, that maybe I haven't robbed her (or my father) of the thing that seems to matter most. "She'll get those skills back, right?"

"Perhaps." The nurse pauses. "First, though, her brain must work correctly, in order to tell her body what to do. We'll just have to wait and see, honey bun."

Why must she call everyone these annoying names?

"But my sister's an amazing athlete," I argue. "Doesn't that count for anything? Nellie *was* . . . I mean, she *is* . . . a champion."

"A champion?" Grace's pen is poised over the chart. "Good. That means she already knows a thing or two about fighting. She'll need that."

The nurse hangs the chart on the edge of the bed and marches out into the corridor. Without giving me the answer I really wanted to hear.

My father peers out the window. On the street below, I can hear the sudden shriek of an ambulance siren. The sound instantly brings me back to that horrible night. Dad seems bothered by it, too.

"We need to talk, Claire," he says sternly. "I hope it's understood that you're not to see Nick anymore—or Adam. Or any of those kids who were at the party last week."

What? Is he serious? He can't keep me from seeing my friends. Nick has been talking me down off the ledge every day—I'm not strong enough to break up with him now.

My mother looks surprised, too. "What are you saying, Jim?"

"Well, our own daughter didn't tell us, but apparently her boyfriend is the one who arranged the party. And I just found out that Adam Silva used his boat to deliver those kegs."

I feel suddenly sick. "I wanted to tell you guys. There hasn't been a chance!"

That's not completely true, and my father looks like he knows it. It's so wrong keeping secrets from them. What kind of person have I become? And what am I supposed to believe? Nick thinks Adam made a deal with the cops so that everyone else would get in trouble. (To me that doesn't sound like Fish.) But after what I've done, it seems crazy to judge Adam. And I don't want my father judging him, either.

"It's not Adam's fault we had the accident. He's a good kid, Dad. You know that. He stayed with us until the ambulance came."

"Good kids don't get arrested, Claire. The police are pressing charges against the lot of them—serving alcohol to minors. They all might go to jail."

"What? No, they won't. Nick said his lawyer will get him off. He just made *one* bad decision. He told me to tell you he's really sorry."

"He's *sorry*? 'Sorry' doesn't even *begin* to cut it. *Three* kegs, Claire? Apparently, a lot of bad decisions were made that night."

He looks at me accusingly.

"I told you I wasn't drinking. I only had one sip of beer!"

"Well, your blood test will answer that. But you shouldn't have been drinking at all. Don't forget, you lied to us, too. You told us you were going to the movies, and you didn't. And what's worse, you dragged your sister along with you. We trusted all of you kids. You, Nick, Adam. Obviously, we shouldn't have. But none of it matters now, does it? Look at your sister. Just look. It's too late."

He'll never forgive me for this.

"Dad, I said I was sorry. *Please.*"

Mom interrupts us. "Stop it. Both of you. Nellie can hear you!"

Over in the bed, my sister's battered face twists into a grimace. She rolls her body onto the side, almost curling up into a ball, and begins to moan.

"Home. Wanna go hoooome." Nellie's voice is hoarse, strained, like a high-pitched, squeaky whisper.

I want to run out of the room—but I can't seem to move.

"You're not ready to come home yet." Mom tries to console her, stroking her hand. "You've been in an accident. But we can't wait for you to be back where you belong. Right, Jim? Claire?"

I don't exactly know how to answer this, because the person lying there hardly resembles my sister. Or at least not the sister I thought she'd be when she finally came out of her coma. This isn't what happens in the movies—at least not any movie I ever saw. And truthfully, I don't think I want this sister to come home with us—*ever*. This sister is just a banged-up imposter with a strange, creepy voice and a bolt in her brain and half her hair shaved off and . . . what have they done to her beautiful hair!?

"Maaaa," she cries, squeaking out the words. "Not like it here!!" Her eyes are unfocused. Her leg (the one not in a cast) moves up and down spastically. With her left arm, she bats at something unseen.

Oh my god. Oh my god. Oh my god.

It's too much. Way too much to take in. It's unbearable to look at her. And what's worse, the worst thing is . . . that she is this way because . . . of *me*.

What the hell have I done?

Mom stares at me. "Claire? Are you okay?"

"No. Feel sick. Gotta go."

I run out of the room and push my way through the hall, but it's crowded with visitors and wheelchairs and tall racks of disgusting-smelling food trays. It's a maze of endless corridors and nurses' stations and double doors leading anywhere but where I want to go—which is the hell out of here!

Completely confused, I approach a random group of people who are standing near a coffee machine. "The elevator? Have you seen it?"

(Only the most pathetic question ever asked.)

A bearded man in a lab coat takes pity on me. "Two lefts and then a right down that hall."

I spin around, but as I do, I practically crash into Nellie's nurse, Grace, who is leaning over a pushcart full of test tubes.

"Slow down, baby doll. We don't need you getting hurt, too."

"It's Claire," I mutter, trying to get around her.

She takes one look at my face and stops me. "Oh, honey bun. Wait." She pulls a crumpled blue tissue out of her pocket. "Something happen back there?"

I don't know why, but suddenly everything inside me breaks apart, like maybe even my soul, if that's possible.

"My . . . my . . . father . . . ," I sob. Heavy, wracking sobs.

"There, there now." Grace gently pats my back. "This is hard, isn't it? Your family is going through a really tough time. Your parents look exhausted. How are *you* holding up?"

I take the tissue from her and blow my nose. "He blames me, my dad. He's right. I was the one driving the car. Don't know if I can come back here. Not till she's better. *Normal.* Will she ever be normal again? I'm sorry. I just can't stand it! It's so hard. Unbelievably hard, to see her this way."

"It must be. But maybe you've just got to be brave."

I stop crying and look, *really look*, at her. Up close, she's still tan and wrinkly, but her eyes are moist and filling with tears, like mine.

And she's got these striking blue eyes, with orange eye shadow, rimmed in black—like a butterfly. Which reminds me, Nellie always loved butterflies; monarchs were her favorite. When we were little, she would trap them in old peanut butter jars—that is, until I'd yell at her, *Let them go, dummy. If you don't they're gonna die!*

(I haven't always been the nicest sister.)

The nurse smiles. "It's only hard because you love her."

What? How does she know this?

"Of course you love her. She's your sister, right? Her injury doesn't change that. *Nothing* will change that."

I gulp back another sob. "But what if . . . I can't . . . ?"

"Can't what?" Grace shakes her head. "It won't be easy. In fact, it might be the hardest thing you'll ever do. But you'd better suck it up, buttercup—because your sister is definitely going to need you."

SID

Claire calls and says she needs me—to take her to the senior graduation. My grandmother lets me borrow her van, only if I promise not to leave the tank on empty like last time. Lord, for somebody her age, she doesn't miss much. So after lunch, I drive over to the Perrys'.

When Claire comes out, she tells me her parents are spending the afternoon at the rehabilitation center near Boston, where Nellie was transferred a couple of weeks ago. I notice my friend is wearing makeup for a change. Her navy blue halter dress is nice, and she's even straightened her hair.

"Do you mind not seeing Nellie today?" I ask, since that's the main reason she's given me lately for not wanting to hang out.

She climbs into the van. "Not really. It gave me a good excuse *not* to, Sid."

What the heck? "Sorry, but isn't that kind of harsh?"

"Could we drop it? You don't understand how stressful it is." She adds, "Seeing her that way."

I want to say, *Yes, I do. Your sister is my friend, too!*

Who does she think went with her to the hospital to say good-bye? Thank God Nellie made it, but how awful was that? If *anyone* would understand, it's me.

I've been through a lot myself.

It's not so much fun without a father around, but I'm not one to complain. And it's way stressful to visit my mom in that crazy group home. But I never opt *not* to go.

Of course, I don't say any of this, because here's the thing: Claire has changed since the accident—she's unpredictable, unhappy, *un*-Claire. Adam's noticed it, too. She's avoiding him—big time. I told him last night that she's not exactly hanging with me, either. She's not allowed to see *anyone* from the party, but he's decided to take it personally.

Poor Adam. He sounded so bummed.

It's a beautiful, clear-sky day. When we get to the high school, we find a seat near the top of the bleachers. Metal chairs have been set up on the football field for the ceremony. Everyone in the stands is excited. Families are all dressed up and sitting together, taking pictures and applauding. As our principal reads off their names, kids walk across the stage to receive their diplomas.

"Abhishek Fando."

"Emily Flanders."

The graduates are all happy-happy today. I guess they're celebrating the reason they wrote all those papers and studied for all those tests.

But the longer I sit here, the more I realize I'm not looking forward to being on that stage next June, since I can't count on either of my parents being there to see me cross it. Oh, I know, Grams will come, and Miles—and Trey (hopefully), but for some reason, that doesn't seem like enough. And life after high school seems like a scary place to be without parents.

Claire gets out her digital camera from her purse and aims at me. "Smile, Sid. That's gonna be us next year."

After she shows me the picture, I ask, "Do we really have to graduate?"

She gives me an eye roll. "Are you serious? I can't wait to get the hell out of this school."

"*Carol Anne Francis.*"

"*Nicholas Fronchetta.*"

When Nick approaches the podium, Claire stands up and begins clapping like crazy. You'd never know she's been so depressed. As he waltzes up to take his diploma, I've got to give the boy credit. He looks like someone with a bright future ahead of him—not like the possessive psycho who won't let my best friend break up with him (or so she says).

She's made excuse after excuse about it—it's a little sickening.

After she takes some more pictures, Claire turns to me. "Sid, will you bring me to his thing later?" Everyone knows that Nick's parents are having this big-old graduation party for him tonight, but last time I checked, she wasn't sure she wanted to go.

"Are you really up for being around all those people?"

"Maybe not." She pauses. "But I kind of feel obligated. Nick's been so supportive. He's been over my house almost every day after school. Meredith, too."

I'm stunned. I had no idea. She's had them over—but not me?

"But I thought you hated Meredith!"

"I know. I did. But M's different now. I feel sorry for her. She's been so upset over what happened to Nellie."

"Like I'm not? What about your dad? I'm surprised he's okay with them being over your—"

"Well, he *wouldn't* be okay with it, Sid, if he knew. He's always at work. Mom's always in Boston. They have no clue."

She shrugs, like, what else can she do?

I sit on my hands to keep from slapping her. "You know, after all that's happened, I can't believe you're still lying to your parents."

I want to scream, *You don't know how lucky you are to even have parents!*

She shrinks away from me. "I'd tell them the truth, Sid. But I don't think they can handle it."

Which makes me wonder—how much of the truth has she been telling any of us these days?

She forces a painful smile. "So, can you take me, Sid?"

Like the sucker I am, I agree.

The Fronchettas live in a minimansion with tall glass windows and a stone wall surrounding the entire property. The sun is setting as we get there, and people are streaming up the lawn that's velvety green and as groomed as a golf course. And, believe it or not, a white-gloved chauffeur directing traffic tells me where to park along the street.

Claire and I walk up the long driveway and around to the backyard where they've set up this huge white party tent. Hundreds of tiny lights are strung everywhere; I have to admit, it looks beautiful.

Most of the people we run into are being nice (not bombarding Claire with too many sensitive questions). After we say congratulations to a few seniors, we get a glass of fruity punch and circulate.

Of course, it doesn't take long for Meredith to find us. She's wearing a short, yellow backless dress that make her shoulder blades stand out. *Twig.*

"Oh, Nicky and I just *knew* you would come, Claire. Thanks for bringing her, Sid."

Claire smiles, but I want to gag on a mini-hot dog that I plucked off a waiter's tray. "That's me," I reply, "Claire's new chauffeur."

Sweet relief when, after a minute, Meredith says she has to go to use the bathroom. After she walks off, Claire grabs my arm and says, "Let's go find Nick."

Her stupid boyfriend is standing next to his father, a balding guy with ruddy cheeks, near the bar. We say a quick hello to Mr. F., but then he has to take care of a "running-out-of-ice" emergency.

"Hi." Nick pulls on Claire's waist, bringing her close. "I didn't think you were going to make it, baby."

"Sid talked me into it," she replies, which obviously isn't true.

"Good old Sid," Nick says. "How's things?"

Before I get a chance to answer, his hand is on my back,

and he's steering both of us toward the rear of the tent.

"Come on, ladies," he says. "The *real* party's out here."

Nick leads us down a narrow gravel path and through the woods behind his house. I'm hoping there's no poison ivy. At the bottom of the hill is a marshy inlet that leads to the bay. Tied to the wooden dock are the Fronchettas' two Jet Skis, bobbing in the shallow water. One is black with a yellow stripe. And at least fifty kids are standing around the dock with plastic cups in their hands.

What the heck?

"Really, Nick?" I give him the evil eye. "Tell me you don't have a keg back here."

Nick laughs. He reminds me of a monkey when he laughs.

"My old man got it for us, Sid. So relax. We're being safe. I've got to take everybody's car keys or they can't drink at all. Zero. Now, can I get you girls anything?"

"I'm good," I reply nervously. Grams keys aren't leaving my purse.

"Yeah, you're driving. But Claire wants some, right?"

She gives him a little nod.

Crap. I can't believe it. Pulling her aside, I try and talk some sense into her. "You're not seriously going to party tonight?"

"Why not? Don't look at me like that."

"Well, somebody's got to! How can you even want to *be* at another keg party? After what happened last time? And I thought you were breaking up with Nick? I mean, after what he did to Adam? He's got anger issues, Claire. And don't you think drinking might be kind of disrespectful to Nel—"

I can't even get out her sister's name before she starts flipping out.

"*Shut up*, Sid. Can't you just mind your own business? For a change? Nick is one of the few people in this town who isn't judging me. Him and Meredith. Besides, don't you know how hard it is to pretend I'm doing okay? I'm the one who has to live with it. Maybe if I get buzzed, I can forget for a while. Maybe I *need* to forget. Why can't you understand that?"

Why can't *she* see the connection?

And what did she mean by mind my own business—*for a change*? I've barely said two words to her since this whole mess began—because she asked me not to. If that's not minding my own business, what is?

"Here you go." Nick interrupts us with Claire's beer. Then he taps his cup with hers and says, "Here's to Nellie coming home soon. By the way, how late can you girls stay?"

"Actually," I reply, "I promised I'd get the van back early. My grandmother has to work tonight."

"What?" Claire's eyes fly open. "No she doesn't."

"Well, yes she does. She texted me a minute ago." (I figure if my friend can twist the truth, I can, too.)

"Your grandmother texts?" says Nick, impressed.

"Who cares, Nick?" Claire is furious. Nick backs away. "You can't just leave me here, Sid. You know my parents won't let me go to parties anymore. They don't even know I'm here!"

If she wasn't so obnoxiously using me, I could almost feel sorry for her.

She tries again. "Everyone's already started partying. How am I supposed to get home?"

"Well, you could try asking someone who isn't. Oh, look. Isn't that your new best friend, Meredith? Right over there?"

"Don't do this, Sid." She's almost on the verge of tears.

"Fine." I keep forgetting how unstable she's become. "What if we stayed like ten more minutes, okay?"

She hesitates, long enough for Nick to interfere.

"Problem, ladies? Let's sidebar, Claire." They go over to where Meredith is standing for a few minutes, then Nick heads over to the keg, and Claire comes back to me.

"All set," she says, which is kind of a nice surprise, because I didn't want to stay for even one more minute, never mind ten.

"Okay, that's great. Let's go." I start for the path, but she's not following. "What? Do you need to say good-bye to Nick?"

"No, Sid. I meant, I've decided to stick around."

That's when I notice Meredith waving her over. "Hurry up, Claire. The boys are going to start playing strip poker in the boathouse. It'll be hilarious." Meredith smiles at me smugly.

Excuse me? What's happening here? We've been to lots of parties before, but my friend has never completely ditched me—not like this. Not for Meredith. She'd always agree to leave if I had to go.

But Claire is defiantly draining her cup, like there's no way she's about to go now. "Sid, weren't you in a big hurry to leave? Didn't you say your grandmother needed the car?" Her eyes are so cold. I can't believe she's acting this way.

"You've changed since the accident," I say, finally. "I was only trying to help."

"Well, you're not the same, either. So stop trying to help me, okay? You have no idea what I need." With that, she turns and walks off with Meredith. They link arms together, and I can even hear them laughing.

I'm so upset that I run and stumble up the dark path, through the creepy woods and around the outside of the tent, and down the long grassy lawn to our van.

But as I drive away, a part of me feels worried about leaving my best friend on her own tonight. I mean, what if something bad happens to her? Meredith won't look after her like I do.

Then again, I'm starting to wonder if maybe Claire's not actually my best friend anymore. And if that's the case, then maybe it's not my business to try to help her. Maybe nobody can.

GOOD MUSIC IS GOOD MUSIC, AND
EVERYTHING ELSE CAN GO TO HELL.
—*Dave Matthews*

ADAM

Nobody's around to help me. As usual. I'm breaking for lunch. My clothes are full of paint, so I throw a sheet of plastic over Pop's corner of the couch before I sit down. When I flip on the TV, *Nathan's Annual Coney Island Hot Dog Eating Contest* is on ESPN. They hold it every year, Fourth of July (my mother's birthday). Note to self: Call after lunch to avoid guilt trip later.

My father is in his bedroom, asleep. He always sleeps through the Fourth of July. And the fifth. *Too many bad memories*, he says. When my mom was visiting last summer (with cactus-man), Pop's doctor at the VA explained to us that my father experiences a kind of "anniversary reaction" to all of his "trauma."

Too bad trauma can't paint over a garage door that's been sprayed with the word NARC. Ugly black letters—four feet high.

No, that's *my* fun-filled job today.

I discovered the damage this morning. And I'm trying to erase it before Pop wakes up and goes postal on me. The second coat of paint covered it, sort of, so it's more like the word "ARC" (as in Noah's)—but it's definitely still there.

Last week it was our trash. Somebody ripped it open and dumped it all over the front lawn. Pop thinks it was probably those "goddamn nitwit teenagers" and I have to agree. It looked like a freaking landfill out there, with seagulls circling and random brochures from colleges pasted up against tree trunks. It took me hours to clean it all up.

I've decided that Nick is trying to kill me in stages.

Cookie thinks we should retaliate. "We could totally take them, man. We just need a plan." But I'm not biting. I'm in more than enough trouble already, thanks just the same. (And I've also grown somewhat fond of my head.)

My TV show is over. Since I've already inhaled two sandwiches, I should get back to painting those doors. But it's hot, and I'm tired, and I don't feel like painting. Or unloading the dishwasher. Or taking out the recycling. Or doing any of the other chores I'm supposed to do because my dad has temporarily checked out of life, *again.*

It doesn't help that yesterday was my juvenile hearing. For someone who'd "spent a few nights in jail," my father was totally freaked out by the whole ordeal—changing his shirt like three times before we left. Honestly, I was somewhat freaked myself.

We met my lawyer, Pat McCoy, in the parking lot, and then we walked into the Town Hall, up the carpeted staircase, and into the "designated hearing room." Detective Burton was there and two town council members, a youth advocate, and Mr. Martin from school—all sitting around this ten-foot-long, "serious-business" wooden table.

First, they read the charges against me, and then the youth advocate asked, "Adam, do you have anything to say for yourself?"

Actually I had quite a lot to say, but I kept it brief, like Pat had suggested.

"I'm very sorry about what happened. I realize now how many lives I put in jeopardy by my actions. There's no excuse. I just didn't think. So, I guess, if you have to, throw the book at me, okay? I deserve it."

Things got quiet for a minute and then Detective Burton told them how cooperative I'd been with the investigation. After a brief recess, they decided to reduce the charges against me. Oh yeah, I'll have a curfew for six months and random breathalyzers, but no jail time. Pat McCoy told us afterward that they couldn't tie the keg to the accident because Claire's blood test confirmed she wasn't drinking, which means the Perrys can't sue us, either. (Not that I thought they would, but my father was worried.)

So all in all, Pop and I both walked out of there feeling very, very relieved.

Too bad that good feeling won't last. For some reason—using my life's conversion calculator—the balance of good never seems to outweigh the bad.

After a shower, I head outside, past those sorry garage doors, through our dandelion-covered field, and sit by the water. It's hot this afternoon, a regular "steam-ah," as Pop's friends at the docks like to say. I bet the bay will be crowded this afternoon for the holiday.

In Bristol, one town over from us, they hold the annual

Fourth of July parade. It's supposedly the oldest parade in the country—although I've never been.

I remember my mom *wanted* us to go once on her birthday. My baby sister, Molly, was tiny, like three months old. I was six or seven. But I guess Dad had forgotten all about it. They were fighting. I think Mom was yelling because of that—and he was yelling because he'd made other plans.

Anyway, my dad finally slammed out, roaring away in his truck, which meant we couldn't go anywhere, 'cause we didn't have another car. When I went into the kitchen, Mom was crying. She asked me how I'd feel if we left my father. "What do you mean?" I asked. "Like for the night?"

"No. For a lot longer."

That really scared me. But then, after lunch, my dad pulled up in this brand-new (new to us, anyway) light blue convertible.

Mom ran outside with Molly in her arms. I ran out there, too.

"What did you do, Jack?" Mom was so excited. "I can't believe it!"

"You're gonna need it now, with two kids," he said, winking. "Happy Birthday." My father was so proud, the proudest I've ever seen him.

"You idiot," my mother said, teasing. "I thought you weren't coming back."

"I'm not that crazy," he said, hugging my mom. "It's never too late to do the right thing, huh?" He kissed Molly on her head, and he rumpled my hair. "Remember that, buddy, okay?"

We never did make it to the parade, but that was one happy time with my family. Unfortunely, it's the last one I remember.

On the river, there's a droning buzz as a kid rides by on his Jet Ski. I decide to have my nicotine fix, here on the dock. I'm up to half a pack a day now, but who's counting?

Claire and Nellie live on the other side of the river. Not in any of the houses I can see, more like down the street, three blocks in. I've been thinking a lot about what happened to Nellie, especially since Sid and I took a road trip to the rehab center about ten days ago.

Of course, Sid checked with Claire's mom beforehand, to make sure that Mr. Perry wasn't going to be around. Supposedly Claire and Sid are in some kind of a fight—so that's why she didn't come with us. Or maybe she's still avoiding me. Or who knows what the real reason could be?

All I can say is that Nellie isn't exactly Nellie anymore. I mean, at first, she seemed all excited we were there, but when we tried to talk to her, something was off. She kept repeating herself and got frustrated so fast. Out of nowhere she started cursing and crying. After that, her social worker came in and said, "You kids might want to come back another time."

So we left. I was pretty much depressed on the way home. Sid was going on (and on) about how much Claire has changed, and how Claire thinks it's too stressful to visit her own sister. I didn't tell Sid this, but I can totally understand. You see, Sid doesn't have anything to feel guilty about . . . and, well . . . *we* do.

I still haven't talked to Claire. I've wanted to call her. Cookie told me I should call her, but I can't. I'm not sure how she would feel about me calling. Like it might be awkward . . .

considering what I did, what she did—*everything*.

The thing is, sometimes when I'm heading home from that side of town, I drive past the Perrys' house and glance up at the windows upstairs. Nellie isn't home yet, but I try to imagine Claire sitting at her computer or listening to music (or doing whatever it is that girls do in their rooms).

But then I think about Nellie at that rehab and I start feeling bad inside.

I know, when I start blaming myself for what happened, I should really think back to what my father said about finding some good filters—and moving on.

Could Claire be my filter?

I think I'd just settle for her being my friend again.

But I totally don't know how to make that happen. It seems almost impossible now. So I guess that's why I keep driving by her house—for some strange reason, it comforts me.

IN GYMNASTICS, THE LONGEST ROUTINE YOU DO IS A MINUTE
AND A HALF, AND THAT'S PRETTY TOUGH TO GET THROUGH.
—*Shannon Miller*

CLAIRE

For the first time since I was ten, I haven't seen Sid in over a
month. Not since Nick's graduation party. I haven't called
her, and she hasn't called me. Well, she did call once on my
cell—but she didn't leave a message, and so I didn't get back
to her. Whatever. I miss her, but they say sometimes when bad
things happen you find out who your true friends are: the ones
who never judge you.

Still, she was right about one thing. I definitely do *not*
want to drink anymore. Not after hitching a ride home with
Meredith. I can't believe she talked Nick into giving her back
her keys. She was weaving all over the road! How many
chances am I going to get? Besides, partying always makes me
feel worse the next day, *more* depressed—not better. It's been
thirty-three days since I've quit.

(And I'm feeling really good about it, by the way.)

But Nick = partying. Which is one of the reasons I decided
to break up with him, once and for all. I've put him off with
excuses for the past week or so, but for some reason he insisted

on seeing me tonight. After I tell my parents I'm going out for a run, I text him to meet me at the park near my house.

"It's not working," I say as we sit in his Jeep in the twilight, with the streetlights blinking on and the smell of freshly mown grass outside.

"You always say that, baby. Come here." He puts his arm around my shoulder and starts grabbing me. "I've missed you so much."

Why do I have a feeling it wasn't exactly *me* that he missed?

I push his hand away. "Stop it. No, I mean it this time. I can't pretend I'm having fun with you anymore. Why can't you get that? I think we should just be friends."

"Friends with benefits?" he says, raising an eyebrow hopefully.

"A real friend wouldn't ask me that," I reply.

When he finally realizes I'm serious, his face gets all ugly and mean. "Are you just doing this so you can hook up with somebody else?"

I have to laugh at that one. "There's nobody else. It's me. I'm not the same person anymore. Okay? I need a break. And don't stalk me this time, either."

"*Stalk you?*" he replies. "I'm all you've got. But you know what? Maybe Meredith was right."

"Meredith? What did she say?"

"Never mind. I don't want to get you mad."

He's acting all evasive, which makes me wonder if he's been cheating on me with her, behind my back. "It's too late now, Nick. You already started to tell me."

"Okay. Well, I was saying how depressed you've been

lately, like, not wanting to fool around or hang out. And she said I might as well face facts—*you might not ever get over what you did to your own sister.*"

"Screw you, Nick! You and Meredith both!"

I get out and slam the door and run all the way home. I wish I could talk to Sid—or someone, *anyone.* But I've pretty much cut myself off from all my friends. After I mumble goodnight to my parents, I go up my bedroom, climb into bed, and stare at the ceiling. As much as it hurt to hear it, I think Nick was right.

What's wrong with me?

I'd rather be alone. I can't stand to be alone. Because of Nellie.

She's always there, pulling me into her orbit, just like before. There's no escape, even when I finally fall asleep. It's strange, but in my dreams she's okay, not brain-injured, just normal. She's so normal that sometimes, when I wake up, I half expect her to be asleep in the room next door. But she's not. Not yet. I can't imagine how it will be when she comes home.

That was a week and a half ago. This morning, around nine-thirty, I drag myself out of my room, cranky and tired from another restless night. It's not any better when I get downstairs and my father starts nagging me. He doesn't want to keep paying our gymnastics dues when I haven't been back to the club—not even once.

"If you don't want to practice, that's fine. Just make a decision, Claire. By the way," he adds, "it's not helping your mother, this sitting around, punishing yourself. Doesn't she have enough to deal with? It's actually kind of selfish. Did you hear me, Claire?"

"Okay then, could you take me? To the gym? Today?"

He blinks, probably surprised that I listened to him for a change. Mom is going to Boston as usual, so Dad said he'll leave the store early to take me.

He arrives home at four, just like he promised. What I didn't count on was him driving us by the scene of the accident. (I always make Mom avoid that road, even if it means going the long way through town.)

He actually stops the car. And suggests I get out. He comes around and opens my door.

"Dad, please. No. Not now."

"You're going to have to face it sometime."

So I get out and walk around. Funny, it's just an ordinary-looking tree in a clump of other trees. You can tell it's the tree I hit, though, because there's this huge, charred chunk of bark missing on one side. But nobody has placed flowers beneath it—or ribbons or photographs, or any of the mementos you might see at the sites of other terrible accidents—because my sister didn't die.

(It only feels that way sometimes.)

Just a few yards beyond the tree is the marshy river, filled with reeds and tall cattails. I hadn't realized how close we almost came to crashing into the water. What might have happened to Nellie then?

Before we leave, my father steps closer. "One more thing," he says stiffly. "We've decided to ask the judge for leniency,

Claire. Your lawyer said if we do, the most you will get, besides losing your license, is some hours of community service. Okay? I hope you realize I don't blame you. As I said before, many mistakes were made that night."

"*Okay,*" I say, but that's all, even though the truth is right there in my head. (It never leaves my head.)

You asked for it, Nellie. Here we go.

I want to tell him everything that happened that night, but I can't. How could I disappoint him all over again?

I'm such a coward.

Besides, it doesn't matter whether my father blames me or not. I blame myself enough for the both of us.

Although everything in my life is completely upside down, our gym looks exactly the same. There are dozens of bright blue mats covering the floor, a row of gleaming trophies in the glass case, and an American flag hung on the side wall. The vault (or horse) sits at the far corner. And the uneven bars stand in their usual spot, with the chalk bucket nearby. Even Melissa's favorite corny saying still hangs over the water-spotted bubbler:

Whatever the challenge
Whatever the test . . .
Whatever you strive for
Give it your best.

When Sid was doing gymnastics with us (for two years during middle school), she and I used to hide that sign as a joke on Melissa—but, the next day, another one with the same saying would always reappear.

It's hot in here, humid, with a dirty-sock smell. The three ceiling fans are on the highest speed, but they aren't helping much. It's late afternoon. Wednesday. Mid-July. A month and a half since the accident—that's how my family measures time now.

I've avoided coming to our club because of what I thought might happen. And it *does* happen.

My sister is all over this place; even her voice haunts me here.

One. Two. Three. Count it out, Claire. It's easy. Come on!

Coach Melissa is in her office at the computer. She's wearing her blue shirt with the Stand It Up logo, a silver eyebrow ring, and her hair (brown with red streaky highlights) is pulled back in a ponytail, which makes her look more like twenty than thirty-five. When she was my age, Melissa had already won the state championships on bars three years in a row—pretty much a legend around here.

"Hi, Claire!" she says, looking genuinely excited to see me. "How's everything? How are *you*?"

"Still breathing," I reply. Then I shrug, because what am I supposed to say, *Sorry I ruined your star gymnast?*

I brace myself for the usual questions: *Any better? Still in Boston? When's she coming home?* But Melissa must have already gotten the update from my parents, because (unlike everyone else in this gossip-hungry town) she doesn't ask.

"Well, breathing is good," she says, putting a stamp on an envelope. "Are you planning to stick around?"

Does she mean tonight or permanently? Because now that she's asking, I'm not exactly sure. I peer into the gym again—no one's around.

"Mostly I just wanted to say hi, Melissa. And my mom wanted me to thank you for calling. Actually . . . do you mind if I practice for a while? I mean, if it's not too late?"

She glances at her watch like it might be. "Okay," she answers. "I have a few more bills I can pay. I'll let you know when I'm finished."

I open the door and walk to the center of the gym. After warming up with some sit-ups, push-ups, and a few stretches, I go over to the high beam, chalk up, and mount.

The balance beam is a mere four inches wide—that's it—but there's soft padding for the balls of your feet. This helps you stay on, sort of. At least Melissa always says so.

Remember, girls. Trust your body. You've been doing this since third grade. Don't think. When you think is when you fall on your head.

I begin with one of my old routines, only ninety seconds long—but it's a *long* ninety seconds. I lift my chin, shoulders square, hands poised, eyes focused on the end of the beam.

Pivot turn. Relevé. Long run to a leap—my toes point in midair.

Nellie was perfection on the beam. She rarely fell, even during practice. *See how straight her legs are in that headstand, girls? That's how your legs should be.*

Things are going along fine . . . when what should have been an easy pivot turn suddenly *isn't,* and my foot falls over to the side. Then, I overbalance. *Wobble. Wobble. Wobble.*

My hands go out. They're not supposed to go out. My arms tighten. They're supposed to relax. *Losing it. Losing it. Concentrate!*

It's always a lack of concentration when you fall.

Okay. *Wait.* I can do this. Start again.

Remount. Toes grip. Switch leap, straddle, then stand.

Visualizing my next move, I pull in my stomach. All toes

on, I lunge. I arabesque. Forward roll. Almost there. Only a few more steps to dismount.

Maybe I could keep coming, I suppose . . . just to practice. But it's hard to focus. I can't seem to shut off my brain.

Wobble. Wobble. Wobble.

Hands out. Balance check.

Damn!

Down and off the beam.

So much depends on not falling. If you fall during a competition, there's no way to recover. The judges lop off points as mercilessly as an executioner might lop off your head. *Deduction! Deduction! Deduction!*

I get up and mount again. Straddle mount this time. Leap from the knee and lunge. *Stay on. Stay on.* Walk s-l-o-w-l-y. Arms extended. Pointed toes. Pivot turn. Prancing back and forth, using the entire length of the beam.

Now for the hard part. My dismount. If I miss it?

I *can't* miss it.

Back-twist dismount. Flying through the air, head away from—never *toward*—the beam. Trying to find my center. *Find it. Find it.*

But then, I come down too hard. Forget to bend my knees. And land smack on my butt!

"Ouch." Melissa has come out of her office. "But considering everything, that wasn't half bad. It's all about focus, right?"

"Focus. Right." I stand up and brush myself off.

"Enough for tonight?" she asks. I nod.

Melissa pulls her office door shut and locks it behind her. She smiles at me. "By the way, did you remember that my second session of camp starts tomorrow? Honestly, Claire, I hoped that was why you came in. I've got sixteen girls signed up. The job's still yours if you want it."

Job? My summer job. Melissa's held my summer job for *me*?

"I can really use you, Claire. What do you say?"

I look around. It feels good to be here. Not great, but better. Actually, that last time on beam I didn't think about my sister for almost two whole minutes, which since the accident must be some kind of a record.

"Okay, Melissa. I mean, yes . . . thanks."

I breathe in the twin smells of chalk and mat sweat and smile.

It's a real mess. It smells. And no privacy, Sid. I mean, how'd you like to take a crap out in the open—front of strangers? And carry it in a poo-bag to the burn pile every day? Dion says, "you didn't adjust yet?" I want to adjust myself right out of here.

—*Trey*

SID

"No black raspberry?"

I'm behind the counter at the Eye-Scream shop with a cold, wet scoop in my hand. Laura is off tonight. Brooke is in the back on her break. We've got two more hours till closing.

"Only raspberry *chocolate chip*, sir," I repeat to this old man, who's stuck on asking for a flavor we just don't have in the store.

"So, it's got chips?" he asks, adjusting his bow tie. "'Cause I definitely don't want chips."

The first day of August. It's been that kind of summer. Rainy on my days off, sunny when I'm here. The customers are mad-annoying. But only a month till Trey comes home!

I'm about to say to the old man: *Can't you just eat around the dang chips?* When, out of the blue, Adam Silva walks into the store. He's wearing grungy-looking jean shorts and a mud-splotched T-shirt, looking like he just got off the boat. Literally. "Hey, Sid," he says.

"Hey!"

Adam checks his phone while he waits behind the man. Fish and I have texted a few times, but we haven't hung out since we visited Nellie at the rehab in June. It's really good to see him. Nice to see *somebody* smile for a change.

I wipe the counter where chocolate jimmies scatter like ants and ask the old man (for the third time) if he's decided yet. "Ready to order, sir?"

He peers into the glass case again. "You got any plain ordinary ice cream? What do you call it again?"

"Do you mean *vanilla*?"

He chuckles and removes a sugar cone from the stack on the counter. "That's it. Thank you, young lady. Fill 'er up!"

He pays for the cone with a pile of change and leaves. Now it's just Adam and me.

"Do you have any ice cream that doesn't have ice cream in it?" he says, his brown eyes teasing.

"Ha-ha," I say, thinking that Fish seems almost like his old self again, which is a sweet relief after everything. He told me about the juvenile hearing board giving him a curfew, so he can't get caught out past eight at night or he'll get in a lot of trouble. More trouble, I mean.

"So, how's it going with house arrest?" I ask.

"Curfew sucks," he admits, "but I hear it's way better than jail."

Brooke comes back from her break, and Adam and I go sit down by the plate glass window.

"So, anyway," he says, "have you heard anything from Claire?"

His eyes search mine like this might be one of the main reasons why he's stopped in here tonight. I wish I could help him out.

"We're in a fight, remember? I told you what happened. Why . . . have you?"

"No." Adam takes a sip of his soda. "I just assumed you'd have found a way to make up with her by now."

It stings when he says it like that—like somehow he's blaming me.

Here's the thing: I *do* miss her. The Perrys are like my second family . . . at least they *were*. Usually, I'd rather spend time with them than with my own family. Or my father, anyway, who is "supposedly" driving all the way up from Miami for my birthday this year. We'll see if that happens.

"I tried, Adam. Claire didn't get back to me. What more can I do? Keep getting kicked in the face?"

"No," Adam mumbles, as if he's had some experience with that.

"Anyway, change of subject. I'm having a party at the end of August when Trey comes home. It's my birthday, too. Can you help out with the music?" I thought of the party just last week, but my mind's been going crazy with ideas ever since.

"Possibly," he replies without much enthusiasm.

"Are you worried about your curfew? What if I make sure it starts in the afternoon?"

"Maybe." He pauses. "Listen, my dad was in a war, Sid. Trey might not even want a party. Or any attention at all. Did you ever think he might be different when he gets back home?"

Why does everyone feel the need to keep telling me that?

Before I can answer, a car at the stoplight outside screeches away. It's a big Jeep. Like Nick's. We both jump, especially Adam.

"Hey, I almost forgot to tell you," I say. "Nick was in here the other night. He asked if I'd seen you. I told him no, of course, which was true. But then he said something about how he was wondering if you were getting all his messages?"

Adam's thick eyebrows knit together. "I told you about the garbage on our lawn, right? And the spray paint on the garage? Well, somebody egged my car over the weekend. And they let the air out of my tires."

Poor Adam. "What is Nick's problem, anyway? I thought his lawyer got him off," I say.

"He did. They all got off. Well, almost everyone. Cookie said he heard R.J. just got out of juvenile detention."

"He heard right." The whole group of them from the party had been here on Wednesday night, celebrating R.J.'s release—Nick, Meredith, Trevor, Chris Hawkins. And from how they were talking, they were only just getting started with Adam.

"Don't get me wrong, Adam. But do you ever think maybe you shouldn't have turned them in?"

The chair makes a scraping noise as he abruptly pushes it back from the table. "Whatever, Sid. I gotta go."

"Wait. I didn't mean anything—what's wrong?"

He frowns. "Nick's been giving me grief since middle school. Sometimes you get tired of taking it, you know? I thought I was doing the right thing. But in the end, it didn't matter. It probably made things worse."

"Everything's changed since the accident, Adam. I'm sorry I said that. I don't know the right thing to do or say anymore. It's like we've all been blown apart!"

He takes out his keys. "Yeah, well, it's too late for me, but don't give up. On Claire, I mean. She's been through a lot. You two were best friends—and in life that doesn't happen very often. At least not for me."

Could he be right? Should I try reaching out to her again?

I realize there's something else I need to tell him. "Claire doesn't blame you for the accident, you know."

He looks surprised. "She told you that?"

"Um, no. But obviously what happened wasn't your fault. What she said was that she's the one who has to live with it."

"Actually, we *all* have to live with it," he says quietly, walking toward the door.

"Wait, Adam." I don't want him to leave yet. Not like this.

"Before you go, there is *some* good news," I say, smiling and reaching for his hand. "Nellie's getting discharged next week. My grandmother ran into Mrs. Perry at the grocery store. And did you hear Nick's going out with Meredith again?"

"Seriously?" His face brightens.

"Yup. They were together the other night, all p.d.a. crazy. Which means Claire finally kicked his butt to the curb—or he got rid of her, or whatever."

"Wow," Adam says. "I can't believe it. That is so awesome." He's smiling from ear to ear. In fact, he might be even happier than I am.

And suddenly, it hits me. "Oh, my gosh. You like her, don't you? You never stopped! Don't even try to deny it!" I poke him in the chest.

He fakes an "ouch" and shrugs. "Yeah, but is that too weird? I mean, I sort of went out with Nellie."

"So? I had a crush on Trey's cousin before I met Trey. I think you should definitely go for it."

He looks out the window and shakes his head. "You make it sound so easy. Are you forgetting she isn't even talking to me anymore?"

"Oh, right. There's that." But I'm also thinking with Nick out of the picture, Claire might be pretty lonely.

Heck, she might even *need* us. Even if she won't admit it.

"Listen, Adam. I have an idea. I know she finally started working at the gym—one of Nellie's friends told me. Maybe we could go over there together, some afternoon next week, and sort of kidnap her. It might be hard for her to say no to both of us."

"You would do that for me?"

For *him*?

"I'd do anything to get things back the way they were. I really miss her. And Claire's got to be missing us, too. Nellie's not the only one who was hurt that night."

He nods like he knows *exactly* what I mean.

BLAST MEDICINE ANYWAY! WE'VE LEARNED TO TIE INTO
EVERY ORGAN IN THE HUMAN BODY BUT ONE. THE BRAIN!
THE BRAIN IS WHAT LIFE IS ALL ABOUT.
—*Dr. Leonard H. McCoy*

NELLIE'S BRAIN

Aide in his blue scrubs brings a wheelchair into the room, although Nellie can walk now with a cane. Whenever anyone gets discharged from the Rehabilitation Facility, they must exit in a wheelchair. There are plenty of good reasons for this policy.

"Can't risk her falling, now," Aide says, chuckling. "Might hit her head."

Pardonnez moi if I do not share his sense of humor. However, the Aide is correct. It is a well-known fact that people with TBI are at a greater risk for reinjuring themselves after they leave the safety of a controlled environment.

And our Nellie is going Home at last.

Mother helps her daughter change from her hospital gown into a white cotton shirt and a pair of shorts. She brushes Nellie's short blonde hair and clips the sides with barrettes. Holding up a mirror, she says, "See? Your hair looks wonderful, sweetheart."

"No. Looks dumb. Hate it."

Ahem. Besides the new hairstyle, there was also a bit of

a battle in selecting Nellie's "going home" outfit. Our girl had wanted to wear a sweater and long pants. She insisted. Mother tried to explain that although it is cold in the facility, it is sweltering outside. "You'll be uncomfortable on the way home."

Unfortunately, Nellie had *un problème* understanding this concept. There continues to be a wide gulf between what I know and what I can get her to understand. Dr. Franks says we need to rewire those earlier connections, and the only way we can do that is through repetition. Frankly, Dr. Franks, I am becoming most impatient with this process—and so is Nellie.

"Ef-fing cole in here, Ma," she says angrily. "Why you forget my pants?"

Mother sighs. "I didn't forget them. I just told you."

"No, you didn't." Nellie shakes her head. "No!"

"Stop it. What did we say about screaming?"

Mother glances at Head Nurse, a Latina Woman with dark cascading hair and purple glasses, who has come into the room. They exchange knowing glances.

Together they gather the last of Nellie's things into a clear plastic bag. There are many items to pack: get well cards (a dwindling trickle of them), two pairs of sneakers, photographs, trophies, gymnastics posters—and anything else that might have reminded Nellie of home.

Finally Nellie gets into the wheelchair. Head Nurse opens the door and steers her out of the room. They stop at the circular Main Desk with all the monitors and computers, where the Staff smile and want to shake her hand.

"We'll miss you, Nellie. Good-bye!"

She hurries them through the process. "'K. Bye. Let's go."

Frankly (like Mother), I am a bit nervous about this next transition, but (like Nellie) I am not the least bit sad to be leaving this place. It has been a long six weeks of relearning-how-to-walk therapy, cutting-food-with-a-knife-and-fork therapy, using-soap-when-you-shower therapy, memory cards, computation skills, following directions, identifying common objects, and every other kind of sadistic torture (I mean, *therapy*) you can imagine.

It will not stop after we get home, either. They have already made arrangements for a day rehabilitation program in Providence.

On va vraiment s'amuser. What fun!

After Mother signs off on the discharge instructions, we are wheeled over to the elevators. In the hallway, Janitor, with his short silvery hair, nods from behind his mop and sudsy pail. I am acutely aware of the strong ammonia smell. Nellie wrinkles her nose. He salutes her with one hand on his mop.

"It won't be the same around here without you, cutie. Good luck."

(Why do I have a feeling we are going to need it?)

Mother and Head Nurse are making small talk about the weather when the elevator opens to our floor. Nellie mimics the sound, *"Ding."* The Nurse waits behind Nellie's wheelchair so Mother can enter the elevator first. But somehow she misses the cue that it is *her* job to turn and hold the door.

The door bumps sharply against the wheelchair. Mother gasps.

A startled Nellie throws up her arms. "Tryin' to kill me, bitch?"

Mother flinches. "What did you say?"

Nellie hides her face. "Sorry, 'K?"

Progress update: It is not uncommon for patients to be "disinhibited" during this phase of recovery, cursing at inappropriate times or not following social norms, all of which can be quite upsetting for those around them.

The Nurse puts a hand on Mother's shoulder. "It'll get better. You'll see."

Nellie looks up at them. "What'll get better?"

They answer together, "Never mind."

The elevator doors open again, and we arrive on the first floor. Nellie is wheeled past the Visitor's Lounge, past the gleaming wood tables, the plastic flower arrangements, the sectional sofa, and the patient "orientation" sign. On a large, white Dry-Erase board is written the following:

TODAY IS FRIDAY. AUGUST 3RD. LUNCH: CHICKEN PATTIES.
IT IS SUNNY OUTSIDE.

I am silently celebrating the fact that I will never have to see that moronic sign again. As we are pushed through the automatic exit door, I observe that it must be over ninety degrees outside. In the parking lot, the automobiles have that "wavy" air above their hoods. But despite the blast of sticky weather, it feels wonderful to be outside, breathing noninstitutionalized air.

(*Mes amis,* there are things to be grateful for in *every* situation.)

"This your car, Ma?" says Nellie as they stop in the middle of the row behind a light blue Camry.

"Yes. We had to get a new one, remember?"

Nurse helps Nellie into the passenger side as Mother says her final good-byes. "Thank you again for everything. I can't believe she's ready to go home."

"We're always here if you need us," the Nurse replies. "Just take it slow."

How else would we be expected to take it?

After that, Mother pops the trunk and throws Nellie's bag inside. Then she opens her door and gets behind the wheel. "All set, honey?"

"No. NO!" Fumbling, Nellie unbuckles her seat belt. "Switch seats. I want to drive. 'K, Ma?" Her hand reaches out, gripping the wheel.

Mother looks distressed. "Oh, no. Not today."

"But want to. Have permit, right?"

Mother leans across and refastens Nellie's seat belt. "Not anymore. Listen to me. Don't take that off again."

"Bitch," Nellie mutters under her breath.

"I heard that," says Mother firmly. "Listen. I'm not trying to upset you, Nellie. I'm on *your* side. You lost your permit after the accident. All right?"

"Find it later, 'K?" Nellie answers. Hopeful. Confused.

Mother does not reply.

The Security Guard waves the car through the white gate. As Mother drives out of the parking lot, Nellie lowers the window then raises it. Lowers and raises it. She pushes the button for the radio, too; all the buttons she can reach—the glove compartment, the air-conditioning, the emergency lights.

Finally, Mother loses her patience. "Nellie! Enough! I have to drive."

"'K."

Like I said, I am doing the best I can.

Mother drives carefully past buildings that Nellie recognizes: a gas station, a furniture store, a bank. And before long, she puts on her turn signal and merges onto the highway. We are heading south on Route 95.

Nellie's face is glued to the window. "Where we goin' again, Ma?"

Mother exhales softly. "Home, honey. Remember? I told you. We're going home."

GYMNASTICS IS BASICALLY A COLLECTION OF DIFFERENT
SKILLS COMBINED IN MANY DIFFERENT WAYS.
EVERYTHING YOU LEARN, NO MATTER HOW MINOR IT SEEMS,
WILL LEAD TO SOMETHING ELSE. . . .
—*Make the Team*

CLAIRE

She's home. Reporters came to our house yesterday afternoon. "Gymnast Returns. Rehabilitation Continues."

So, of course, we had a small welcome-back party for my sister—just our family. Mom prepared Nellie's favorite spaghetti dinner, and Nellie seemed to enjoy it, even if it was gross to watch her eating pasta . . . with half of it falling out of her mouth.

S-good, Ma. She piled more onto her spoon.

Don't use your fingers, okay? Good to have you home, honey.

Sure is, said Dad, putting a napkin onto her lap.

Isn't it good to have her home, Claire? Mom repeated, trying to include me. *Just like before?*

Great, I replied, because I *was* happy to have her here— but, sorry, it was nothing even *remotely* like before.

If our house had seemed quiet and strangely empty without my sister, now there almost isn't enough room. Either she's standing or sitting too close to me, or talking too loudly, or poking Sandy, our cat, with her cane. It makes me feel like such a bitch to say this, but this new Nellie is ten times more annoying than the old one ever was! And we can't leave her alone, not for a second.

There are also those embarrassing reminder signs that Mom has taped all over the house. In the downstairs bathroom, one says: RINSE HAIR AFTER SHAMPOO. UNDERWEAR GOES ON FIRST. TOOTHPASTE!

Sort of like child-proofing for a toddler. Last night my hair was dripping wet and I couldn't find the blow dryer because Mom had completely reorganized the area under the sink.

How can a hair dryer be dangerous? I yelled.

Stop being so selfish, Claire! (That was my father, from the den.)

Selfish? Who did he think had been taking care of the house when Mom was in Boston? Unloading the dishwasher? Feeding Sandy? Picking up the slack? Despite what he said that day by the tree, he still blames me.

He always will.

❧

And if all that isn't bad enough, Nellie charges into my room at six-thirty this morning, waving her cane. Lucky for her, I'm already up. She's wearing a pink nightgown, backward, inside-out, with the tag sticking up under her chin.

"Where ya going?" she says, turning up the volume on my clock radio, sitting down on my bed. "Like this song. Good one."

God, did she forget how much I hate loud noise in the morning? I pull on a T-shirt and shorts. "To the gym. Dad's taking me." I bend over and turn the music down.

"'K. Comin' with you. Gonna go practice."

"No. It's Thursday. Mom's bringing you to that new rehab today. And stop bouncing on the bed. You might fall."

She stops momentarily. "Have to practice sometime."

"Well, not today." After I tie my sneakers, I reach for one of the tassled pillows that I like to arrange up against my headboard. Impulsively, I throw it at her—to see if she can catch it. (She misses.)

How can she possibly think she's ready to practice?

"I'm working at the gym now, Nellie. Did Mom tell you? I'm teaching level two's and three's."

"'K. But when ya comin' home?"

"I don't know. I'm going to meet Sid after work. Remember Sid?"

It's hard to predict who—or what—she'll remember; there's no magic formula. Mom says we have to talk slowly and tell her one thing at a time.

Nellie tilts her head and blinks. "Sid? Yeah. She's nice, right?"

Sid actually called me last night, after we hadn't talked all summer—like we weren't in a fight at all. She wanted to welcome Nellie home and asked if she could stop by sometime. I told her it might be best to wait a few days.

Maybe Sid thought I was making excuses, because then she asked if I was still mad at her. I told her no, that Meredith was an idiot, and that I'd finally broken up with Nick—for good this time. She seemed really happy about that, so I asked if *she* was still mad at *me*.

How can I possibly be mad at you, Claire? We've been best friends since fourth grade.

So that's how we decided to hang out after work today.

I'm really glad that she called me, but seriously? Almost anything would be better than coming home and facing my sister.

"Yeah, Sid's nice," I reply to Nellie. *Way nicer than me.*

When my sister gets down off my bed, our cat races to get out of the way. For some reason, Nellie feels the need to touch every single thing on my dresser—my iPod, a bottle of perfume, my rack of earrings, a pen—like they're all vaguely familiar but she needs to make sure.

As I'm putting on mascara and brushing my hair, I watch her out of the corner of my eye. Eventually she stops and peers over my shoulder into the mirror. There is a dime-sized red scar from the trach. tube that marks the hollow of her throat. They gave her a new haircut, but some of it hasn't grown back in yet. There's a patch of fuzz (sticking up oddly) at the top of her part line.

When her eyes meet mine in the mirror, she says, "You're boo-ful, Claire. Not me." Her lower lip quivers.

Please don't start crying. I can't take it if you cry.

"No, you're still pretty, Nellie. Look at your pretty eyes. Your hair will grow back in, you'll see." I try to brush it down for her, but it's not happening. I give up as she twirls away.

"Least my boyfrien' thinks I'm pretty," she says, hugging her arms to her chest.

Huh? Did she meet some random guy at the rehab center?

"What boyfriend? Who do you mean?"

"Adam. He still likes me, right, Claire? 'Member Adam?"

I groan inwardly. "You still like *Adam*?"

I guess Fish and Sid visited Nellie last month (at least that's what Mom told me)—so obviously Adam's still a friend to my sister. But who knows what he's feeling about me these days? Probably not such good things, since I totally blew him off. Him and everyone else.

It breaks my heart that Nellie thinks he might be her boyfriend. I'm pretty sure that nobody "normal" will go for her now. And the doctors can't tell us how close to normal she'll ever become.

Don't get me wrong, she's making progress. Dr. Franks said that every milestone for a brain-injured patient can be a triumph of sorts, but it's usually not enough for most families—we just keep wanting more. Which makes me feel even worse about being jealous of her . . . *ever*.

God, what a loser I am.

In the mornings, Melissa and I always try to help the girls learn their individual routines. Today I'm paired with one of my favorites, Samantha, and some of the other skilled kids—so time flies by super fast.

After we take a lunch break, the afternoon is spent going over basic skills, or progressions. The girls (all age nine or ten) gather around us on the mat. We're doing forward rolls. Most people think forward rolls are easy, but there's a very specific way gymnasts are taught to do it. They're considered one of our "foundations." *Everything* builds from there.

Melissa is in the middle of explaining when one of the new girls, a kid nicknamed Tiny, interrupts *again*.

"I know! I know! I can do it!" Her pudgy arm shoots up in

the air. Unlike the other girls, who are wearing black practice leotards, she's got on a faded red hand-me-down. (There's always one in every class.)

Nothing bothers Melissa more than being interrupted. "Yes. I'm sure you can, Tiny. Just let me finish—"

"But . . . but . . . I'm an expert!"

"Fine." Melissa forces a smile. "If you insist. Why don't you demonstrate for us? Go ahead, Tiny. We're waiting now."

The girl does it all wrong, of course. Her wobbly roll is crooked—more like a flat tire. Yet, when she's finished, she smiles up at us proudly. "See?"

I arch an eyebrow. "Not so much."

"That's not quite it," Melissa agrees, shaking her head.

There's a pause, and Samantha adds, "Maybe you could try actually *rolling* next time?"

Everyone laughs. I've got to admit, that was pretty funny.

"Shut up!" Tiny yells. She sticks out her bottom lip, like she's going to cry.

"Okay, that's enough!" Melissa claps her hands and glances in my direction. "Bring her over to the other mat, Claire."

Oh joy. "But *Melissa*—"

"For as long as it takes. Tiny? You go with Miss Claire."

The girl picks up her water bottle and follows me, begrudgingly, to the back of the gym. I'm not happy about it, either. But, I realize, the faster she gets this, the faster I can get back to the girls who actually have potential.

"Okay, let's try it again," I say. "Put your chin to your chest. Like this."

"No, thanks. I'm tired. I'm taking a break." She actually lies down on the dusty mat with her arms folded beneath her head. "What time is this over again?"

Unbelievable. Who does she think she is?

"Come on. Sit up. You have to at least try."

"No, I don't. And you can't make me."

"Look, if you don't want to learn gymnastics, why are you even here? What's your problem, anyway?"

"*My* problem?" she says, glaring. "Maybe I don't really want to learn gymnastics. But even if I did, *you* sure don't want to teach me. So stop trying to act like you do, okay?"

"Whatever," I say, but for some reason this really bothers me. Maybe because she's kind of right.

"Wish my mom didn't sign me up at this stupid place," she adds, sighing.

As Tiny examines her fingernails, I think about what Sid and I might do after she comes to pick me up at four. Shop? Go for coffee? Hang out at her house?

After a few minutes, I see that Melissa is opening the pit behind the vault. That's where we keep the soft mats for landing. I run over and ask if I can please, *please* help with vault, because Tiny is being impossible.

Thankfully, Melissa says yes, although she's not completely letting me off the hook. I still have to work with Tiny tomorrow—and the next day, until she gets it. But I'm not going to worry about that right now, because after the beam, vault is one of my favorites.

Speed is what you need most when you're approaching the vault. That's what gives you the most power when you jump off the springboard, which in turn gives you the most air. Nellie was explosive on vault—she used to get what we call *giant* air.

Coach asks me to demonstrate, so I chalk up with just the right consistency (not too pasty), take a long run, and do a

Yurchenko with a twist and a half. I easily stick the landing, then, being silly, I fall backward into the pit behind me.

The girls all clap and cheer. "Yay, Miss Claire!"

(It's fun to have them clapping for *me* for a change.)

Then Melissa instructs them in technique. She says they need to jump hard off the springboard, put their hands onto the vaulting table like they're doing a handstand, and push off. She will be there to spot them.

"Don't slow down," she reminds them. "Keep your eyes on me, and run as fast as you can."

My job is to let the girls know when it's safely their turn. Most of them are trying their best except for you-know-who. She's standing at the very end of the line. Well, actually, she hasn't moved from the end of the line—in about fifteen minutes. (I think I know how she feels.)

At four feet high and five feet across, the vault (or horse) can be extremely intimidating—and, as every gymnast knows, there's about eighty long feet of runway to change your mind. Unfortunately, some of the other girls have noticed Tiny's stalling and are starting to tease her, so I pull her aside for a pep talk.

"Listen, Tiny. It's okay if you're scared. Lots of girls have trouble with vault at first."

"What?" she snaps. "I'm not scared! Why'd you say that? I hurt my ankle yesterday. So obviously I can't run fast enough."

"Okay. Let me see." I hold her chubby leg in my hands, turning her ankle to the side, but I don't detect anything wrong. "It looks fine."

"Well, it's not! And I'm dehydrated, too. You people don't

give enough breaks in this place." She marches over to the water bubbler, leans over, and takes a drink. A very, very long drink.

As I follow her, I glance over at vault. The rest of the class is beginning to get the hang of it. They're cheering for each other as they soar up and over. It's a shame that Tiny won't let herself be a part of the fun. Tapping her on the shoulder, I say, "You don't have to try it, Tiny. But let's at least watch them, okay?"

She comes with me, and we sit on the small set of bleachers. Melissa believes that people learn new skills in all sorts of different ways. She's certainly had to help me, lots of times.

"Listen," I tell Tiny, "when I was your age, I was terrible at vault. But Coach believed in me. She made me practice even when I didn't want to."

"For real? But you're so good at it now."

I shrug. "I'm okay. Average. You should have seen my sister. She could totally fly."

I'm remembering how Nellie would charge down the floor on her approach, power off the springboard, and whip her body up and over. Her toes were always perfectly pointed, back perfectly arched. No hops, no steps, always stick-your-landing perfect.

Tiny tugs on my shirt. "What do you mean she could fly?"

"I mean nobody even came close."

Tiny wrinkles her nose. "Well, if she's so great, why isn't *she* here teaching us instead of you?"

Is Tiny the only girl here who hasn't heard about my sister? For a few seconds I can't answer—how could I begin to explain?

"She just can't, okay? But Nellie loved to practice. My sister practiced all the time. So please don't take this for granted. She'd give anything to be in your place."

There's another burst of cheering. "Stick it! Stick it! That was great, Sam!" Samantha just did an amazing pike—totally the best in the class.

Tiny looks at the floor. "Even if I practiced for the next million years, I'll never be *that* good."

I feel sorry for her all of a sudden. She reminds me of someone I once knew . . . someone like *me*.

"Listen, so what if you're not the best? We can still teach you lots of cool tricks. We'll take it real slow, okay? Like progressions. One step at a time."

"You think?" She smiles so widely that I can see her pink upper gums. "I guess I could try learning cartwheels and stuff. But don't even try getting me near that thing." She glances at the vault in mock-terror, hiding her eyes with her hands.

"Okay, I won't. I promise. But listen, when I first started on vault, not only was I bad at it—but I was scared of it, too."

(What I don't tell her is that I'm scared all the time.)

She seems to think about that for a few seconds when I catch her staring at something behind me. "Hey, Miss Claire? Could I ask you something? You have a boyfriend?"

"Not anymore. Why?"

"Well, there's a boy over there—and he's been checking you out."

What?

Nick hasn't called me or texted me or done any drive-bys, like he usually does whenever we break up (like a hundred times a day until he eventually wears me down), but I wouldn't put it past him to show up here three weeks later.

I get up and brace myself. I've made plans with Sid, and I've let her down too much this summer already.

But when I turn around, it's not Nick. It's Sid. It's so good to see her! She's waving at me from the front of the gym near the door. Oh, wait a minute, there *is* a boy with her.

My heart skips a beat.

It's *Adam*. What's *he* doing here?

A GOOD CLAM HOE, SHAPED TO FIT, IS A TOOL NO
REGULAR CLAMMER ALLOWS ANYONE ELSE TO PUT
HIS HAND TO CARELESSLY.
—*Making a Living Alongshore*

ADAM

"Want to ride shotgun?" I ask Claire.

This afternoon, I'd vacuumed the Maxima, clearing out half-empty Gatorade bottles and nasty, week-old sandwich wrappers from Subway. To get out the smoke smell, I even hung one of those strawberry-scented air-freshener thingies on the dash. That's how happy and stoked I was about seeing Claire.

"That's okay, the back's fine," she replies. "Sid's purse is there."

"Whatever." I shrug and flip the seat, and once Claire is in, Sid gets in the front next to me.

As we cruise down the two-lane highway, with some great tunes playing (not to mention *two* pretty girls in my car), I'm thinking this night has real potential—I don't want to do anything to screw it up.

It's hot. My AC doesn't work great so I lower the windows.

"Okay back there?" I ask, glancing in the rearview to

check if that's too much air. And, well, to see if Claire even *wants* to be here, because there was this moment when she first saw me, like hesitation or disappointment—or I don't know what she was thinking. "We could go somewhere else if you want?"

She's twisting her hair to keep it from being blown around. "No. I like the wind. And pizza sounds fine."

"Well, it looks fine," I say. "Your hair, I mean."

Red. Sexy. In-your-face beautiful. But I say *fine*.

She catches my eye in the mirror. "You think? Actually, I'm kind of a mess."

After that awkward exchange, it gets quiet in the car. I guess that's because there's a lot of stuff we *haven't* talked about, like the accident, Nellie—all the stuff that could get in the way of having fun tonight.

Since nobody's saying much, I crank up the music. I love this song from Dispatch that comes on next. It was from their very last concert. I drum on the steering wheel, and Sid begins singing along in perfect pitch. The ending is the best, with the crowd chanting, *"Don't break up. Don't break up,"* because people like me wanted them to keep making great music forever.

"This could be Nick's theme song," says Sid, bringing up one of the elephants in the room. Or car. Whatever.

"Not anymore." Claire manages a smile, which must mean Sid was right. That tool is finally out of her life. (Wish I could say the same.)

"So anyway, Claire,"—Sid turns around—"we were thinking about going to the movies tomorrow. Brooke said that new scary movie is great. Do you want to come?"

"Maybe," she replies, distracted. "Hey, isn't that car getting too close?"

I glance in my side mirror. "What the *hell*?"

It all happens so fast. One minute I'm driving along, when out of nowhere this car, this dark SUV with tinted windows, comes roaring up behind me on the highway. If she turned around, Claire could practically eat off the hood of his car.

Sid screams, "He's trying to hit you!"

"Get back, you asshole!" I yell.

Suddenly we're bumped from behind. What the *goddamn* hell?

I'm not sticking around for it to happen again. I swerve into the slow lane, but so does he. That only leaves the breakdown lane, which I get into—fast. I'm trying to figure out what to do next when the highway gods must be smiling on me 'cause right up ahead there's a rest stop. So I pull into it quickly, thunking hard, right over the curb.

As they fly by us on the highway, I catch a glimpse of Nick, R.J., and Chris Hawkins. They're all leaning out the tinted windows, fists pumped in the air, yelling, "NARC!"

I never knew it was possible to hate anyone this much.

Pulling slowly into the nearest parking spot at the rest stop, I shut off the motor and try to cool down. *Not* easy. Finally I say, "That's gonna be a hard act to follow. Anybody want to go car-jacking next?"

Sid puts a hand on my shoulder. "What idiots. That *so* wasn't cool. Can you believe it, Claire?"

When she doesn't answer, Sid gives me this worried

look, and we both turn around at the same time.

In the backseat, Claire is huddled in a ball with her arms curled over her head, all fetal-position-like. In a voice that's barely audible she mumbles, "It's . . . really . . . hard . . . to . . . breathe. . . ."

SID

Now, I've been around all sorts of "mental health emergencies" because of my mother's problems—like the time she made me chase the quote-unquote purple vampires out of her bedroom closet. Long story. But I don't think Adam has ever seen a girl having a panic attack before.

"Does she need a doctor or something?" he asks.

"Probably not. Listen, Claire. Just try to think about something else."

"Like what?"

"I don't know. Count to ten."

She tries, but her lips are turning white. "One. Two. Not happening, Sid."

Crap. After all our great plans, the night is going to be ruined!

"Adam? Maybe we should just take her home."

"Okay. But I need to check something first." He gets out of the car and walks around to the other side. Suddenly, I hear the tell-tale hissing of a tire about to go flat.

"Sorry, ladies," he says. "This will only take a few minutes . . . hopefully."

Near the restrooms there's a picnic bench where Claire and I can wait. Adam gets the spare tire and jack out of the trunk, and we go sit down. My grandmother believes that every self-respecting female should know how to change a tire. So once Claire's settled, I ask Adam if he needs any help.

"It's all good, Sid," he calls. "But thanks."

As Claire tries to calm down, I watch the traffic drive by. Across the highway, the clouds are piled in layers, like pink, fluffy pillows against a deep blue sheet of sky. After a while, I notice my friend doesn't look as pale anymore.

"I'm feeling better, Sid," Claire says. "But that was so scary."

"They're insane. They're taking this to a whole other level."

"I agree." She nods then glances at where Adam is changing the tire. "But he kind of makes himself an easy target, don't you think? Fish, I mean."

"What are you talking about? He's doing his best to avoid them!"

"Maybe. But what about those license plates? Anyone can spot his car a mile away. He should get rid of them."

How can she be so cold?

"Nice. Should he have to move to another town, too?"

"Of course not." She stares at the highway for a bit, lost in her own little world. "You don't think Nick saw me just now, do you?"

"What difference would that make?"

"I just don't want him to hurt either of you because of me."

We hear Adam grunt as he takes off the bolts. His arm muscles bulge under his white T-shirt. I can't help staring, even though I already have a boyfriend (who I haven't seen in almost a year).

Out of the corner of my eye I notice my friend staring, too. "You have to admit, Claire, our boy Fish is looking kinda hot these days."

She bites her bottom lip, frowning. "Why didn't you tell me he was coming?"

"About that. I was afraid you might change your mind at the last minute. Trey taught me how to play poker, remember? Never show your hand. I thought it might be harder for you to say no to both of us."

"Whatever," she replies, but she's laughing. "How's Trey doing, by the way? Have you heard from him lately?"

Claire hasn't asked me about my boyfriend in forever, which is another one of those things I have to forgive her for, I guess. But even though Trey isn't here, it doesn't mean he doesn't exist. He e-mailed me last week that another guy from their unit was injured and sent home.

"It's a real scary place. I can't wait till he's done with his tour of duty, so he can put all of that bad stuff behind him."

"Well, yeah. But sometimes it's not so easy to forget bad stuff."

She picks off a strip of flaking green paint from the picnic table. "Can I tell you something, Sid? I think I had a flashback just now. It felt so real. Like the accident was happening all over again. And I thought I was getting better."

I had figured that was what her panic attack was about. "You must be glad Nellie's finally home, aren't you? That's got to help. Now we can all hang out together and help take your mind off everything."

"I guess." She seems suddenly uneasy. "My sister's real different, Sid. As in, maybe you won't want to hang out with her, different."

"I know. We visited her in Boston, remember? But I don't care how different she is; I really want to spend time with her. For people who love her, she's still Nellie, right?"

"Uh-huh." Claire looks sort of embarrassed now. "She only got home yesterday. What about coming by next weekend, would that be okay?"

Reaching into my bag, I open my phone. "Let's see. My schedule's pretty tight. Not sure if I can fit that in."

She laughs and punches me lightly on the arm. "You'd better!"

Finally, a glimpse of my old friend returning—I put my arms around her and touch my nose to hers—like when we used to "Eskimo" kiss. "It's so good to see you, sweetie. I missed you so much."

"Me, too. And seriously, you're right. Our Fish doesn't look half bad."

In the parking lot, Adam is almost finished changing the tire. He lifts the small spare doughnut and puts it on the wheel. As he wipes some sweat off his forehead, he waves at us. It hits me how much he's been going through this summer, too. Claire should know she's not the only one who's feeling bad.

"You know, Adam still blames himself—for the accident. He keeps saying how sorry he is, and I keep telling him it's not his fault, but it's like he doesn't believe me. He's even started smoking again. I made him promise to quit, but he said he's just too stressed out right now."

"Too bad. Cigarettes are gross." She pulls her hands through her hair. "But thinking it was *his* fault? That's actually pretty funny."

"Funny?" I say, getting upset with her all over again. "You wouldn't think it was so funny if you bothered to listen to him once in a while!"

"If I bothered to . . . ?" She's practically shouting now. "You have no idea how hard this is, Sid. You weren't there!"

"Okay. You're right. Calm down. Don't you know how much I think about that? How maybe I could've stopped it if I *was* there?"

"That's not what I meant." She hesitates and then sighs. "There's nothing anyone could've done to stop it. No, what I mean is—you don't know the whole story."

"That's because you won't tell me! Isn't that what friends do? You listened to me when I was going through all that stuff with my parents. You've always been there for me. Why won't you let me do the same for you?"

"I can't, Sid."

"You mean you *won't.*"

Adam puts the jack into the trunk. "Ready to go?" he calls to us. "Or do you girls need to finish your . . . um . . . *fight?*"

Crap, I guess he overheard us.

"We're not fighting," I yell back, "just having a loud-ish discussion."

"But it was over *me,* right?" He wipes his hands on his pants—and flexes his arm muscles—joking.

"Of course," I reply. "We can't decide which one of us wants to jump your hot body."

Even Claire has to laugh at that.

"*Sweet*," he says, grinning. "But I only have like two hours till curfew. So if you're serious, we'd better hurry up."

As we start walking toward his car, I'm hoping that we can still have some fun together, salvage something of this crazy night, when I notice that Claire is lagging behind.

"Sid? Wait up, okay?"

Adam is standing there with his car door open. "What's the matter? Are you okay?" he asks.

Claire looks more upset than before. "Do you think we could drive over to the beach for a few minutes?" she says. "It's quiet there. I want to tell you guys something. And after that, I have to go home."

CLAIRE

Clumps of seaweed, lettuce green, have been washed up
on the beach. In front of us, a fisherman stands knee-
deep in the water, casting a line.

We're sitting in Adam's car in the parking lot. I'm in
front with him. He's just told me how sorry he is about
bringing the keg to the party, and inviting Nellie to come
along, and not being able to pull over so we could pass—all
things that didn't cause the accident, but it's relieving, in a
way, to hear him say it anyway.

(Maybe that's a part of why I was avoiding him for so long.)

"It's okay," I tell him. "But please, *please* don't feel
guilty. It really wasn't your fault."

Now they are waiting for me to tell my version of what
happened that night. I want to tell them, I told them I
would, but the words stick like tar in my throat.

Sid is the type of person who hates to be kept waiting.
"Are you going to tell us or what, Claire? Come on. You'll
feel better. Just get it out."

I'm not convinced that's true, but I tell them, almost all of it, anyway.

"Okay. I was really pissed off at Nellie. She had been so annoying all night, and she was drunk, begging me to pass Adam's car. I was the one driving, though—I should've known better. But I turned into a frigging maniac behind the wheel. I lost control. So that's why it's *totally* my fault—and there's nothing anyone can say to make me feel any better!"

"But you just told me not to blame myself," Adam replies softly. "And now you're doing the exact same thing."

"Yeah, Claire. It was a mistake," says Sid. "An accident. You can't move on unless you forgive yourself."

Next to me, I feel Adam's arm touching mine. Did he move closer? I get that tiny flutter inside but push it away—especially when I remember one of the last things Nellie said, before the accident.

Nothing's happening between the two of you, right? I mean if it was . . . if you were . . . I would never . . .

"*Forgive myself*, Sid? Don't you understand? I've always been jealous and mean to my sister—for like my whole entire life. She was always the prettier one, the talented one, the favorite child. Well, my father's favorite, anyway."

Adam glances at me, and I think about what we said that night on the beach. Does he remember it, too? So much has happened since then.

"There's one thing I can't figure out," says Adam. "Why did you girls try to pass me that second time?"

I had been hoping to gloss over that part.

"She wanted to flash you, okay? She had her shirt off and everything. And the truth is, a part of me wanted to give Nellie exactly what she was asking for. I should have been watching out for her, but instead I was hoping that when we did, you'd think she was being an idiot."

I put my head down, unable to look at him. "Or maybe even a slut." I stop myself. "Nice way to think about your own sister."

There's a pause as they let that sink in.

"Well, I've probably thought worse things about my mom," Adam replies, shrugging.

"I'm not crazy about my dad, either," Sid offers.

After that, nobody says a thing—probably because Sid's father barely calls her anymore, and Adam's mom is always nagging him to move to Arizona.

(And neither of them went into hiding like me.)

"Sorry I haven't been around much this summer. But do you guys get it now? The judge wouldn't do it, so I had to put myself in . . . a sort of prison. That's why I can't let myself have any fun."

"Not liking the sound of that," says Sid glumly.

"It depends," Adam replies. "Exactly how long are you planning to punish yourself?"

"For as long as it takes."

"As long as *what* takes?" asks Sid.

"I don't know. For my sister to get better. Come back to normal, I guess."

Adam's leg is jittering, up and down. "But what if she

doesn't? Get all the way better, I mean. That's a possibility, right? Isn't that what the doctor said?"

"You're right. I don't know. Then maybe for the rest of my life. It doesn't seem fair, does it? That *I* would get to have a life, and *she* . . ."

"You can't really believe that!" Sid cries.

Adam bangs his fist on the wheel. "I'll tell you what isn't fair! Blaming yourself for one crazy split-second mistake. Believe me, it won't change a thing. You're not a freak, Claire. You didn't mean for this to happen. None of us did. Besides, do you think Nellie would actually want that? For you to never have a life?"

"I don't know." My voice is cracking. "I just can't . . ."

Sid leans forward and rests her soft hair against my face. "You don't have to go through this alone, you know. Lots of people love you."

"Sorry," says Adam, flustered. "I didn't mean to get you upset."

My eyes are blurry with tears. On the beach, the fisherman has dumped his bucket of bait in the sand. Dozens of seagulls begin to circle overhead as the orange ball of sun melts into the bay.

After a minute, Adam puts his arm around my shoulder. "You know, there are lots of ways to escape from prison. What if we helped you get out?"

"I miss you," Sid adds. "Please let us try."

That sounds so good. No, it sounds more than good. It sounds like hope. Like a tiny beam of a flashlight at the end of this incredibly long and lonely tunnel. My friends—and hope—all wrapped up into one.

"Sort of interesting, though," Adam adds sheepishly. "Your sister really wanted to show me her—"

"Hey!" From the backseat, Sid bops him hard on the side of his head. "Do you always have to be such a *boy*!?"

"Ow!" He turns around. "What the hell else am I *supposed* to be?!"

We laugh for a minute, the special kind of laughter that only happens between good old friends. It's making the unbearable somehow bearable again.

Then all of a sudden, Adam's stomach emits this extraordinarily loud gurgling sound. "Wasn't me," he says, and we all laugh again.

"Is anyone else getting hungry?" Sid asks.

"Yes," says Adam. "Must. Get. Food. *Now.*" He turns on the ignition. "What do you think, Claire? Can you come with us?"

"Someplace close, if that's okay?"

As Adam pulls out of the parking lot, I'm thinking that maybe Sid was right; I do feel better after telling them. But a part of me can't stop thinking that here I am, out with my amazing friends, while my sister is stuck back at home. Most of *her* friends have long since bailed.

Will she ever be able to lead a normal life?

As awful as it's been for me, Nellie must feel like she's

in prison, too. I want to help her escape, but I'm also really scared of trying—because what if I can't?

What if the prison she's in doesn't have a key?

> GOD MAY BE SUBTLE, BUT HE'S NOT PLAIN MEAN.
> —*Albert Einstein*

NELLIE'S BRAIN

"**M**a? Ma? MAAAAAAAaAAAAAA!"

Our girl is upset. *Again.* Although we are getting accustomed to her little "outbursts," she has been home for two weeks. How much longer will she be so boisterous? So destructive?

Status update: The modulation of her emotions continues to be problematic.

Nellie is searching for something in her bedroom. I wish I could assist her, but she is not yet able to access the part of me that manages "location." Therefore, our girl is tearing sheets off her bed, overturning the bookshelf, and pulling her sweaters off the shelf.

Clothes fall from the hangers: Jeans. Dress pants. Skirts. *Toss. Toss. Toss.*

Over to the bed again, she swings her cane. And there goes her clock radio. *Crash, bang.*

Arrête! S'il te plaît!

Stop.

Nellie is also wondering where her Sister has gone. Claire

should be home by now. Claire could help if she were here. Where did she go again?

The pocket spiral notebook which Mother gave her might be of some use in these kinds of situations. Yet, she refuses to use it. (She thinks it is dumb.) But even if Nellie *did* agree to try to write things down, like where her Sister went tonight, she might not be able to remember where she left the notebook in the first place.

Which brings us to the short-term memory issue: It is a problem.

"CAN'T FIND THEM, MAAaaAAAaaaAAAAA!"

Mother is downstairs in the kitchen. Father is working late tonight at the store. That is what Mother said at the dinner table. Nellie does remember that. But where is Claire?

Nellie registers the sound of footsteps on the wooden stairs. Suddenly Mother is standing at the doorway to the room. Her blue-gray eyes squint, taking in the room's destruction. What is that expression on her face?

Worried? Angry? Confused? Upset?

"Nellie? What on earth did you just do?" Her hands are on her hips. "Gosh, darn it!"

Upset.

Nellie begins sobbing in anguish. Mucus is dripping down from her nose; she tastes salty tears. "I can't. I can't. I can't find them."

"Sorry." Mother walks over and gently rubs her back. "Calm down and start at the beginning, honey."

Nellie breathes slowly, opens her mouth, closes it again.

"Can't find my feet," Nellie says, sniffling.

Mother smiles sympathetically. "What are you talking about? Your feet are right there,"—Mother is pointing—"on the ends of your legs. See?"

There is more agitation now as Nellie's heart rate speeds up.

"NO. SAID. CAN'T. FIND. MY. FEET!"

Merde.

Mother is truly perplexed now. "I'm so sorry. I want to help you. Try again, honey. Please."

Nellie bends over and jabs her index finger at one of Mother's blue Dansko sandals. Finally, Mother's eyes light up. She gets it.

"Your *shoes*? You mean your shoes? Is that what you're looking for?"

(Aphasia is the correct term for the difficulty patients have in retrieving the names for common objects.)

Nellie nods vigorously, using a fist to wipe off the tears.

"Your *shoes* are in your *other* closet." Mother walks across the room. "Remember? I labeled them for you and everything. Outside shoes. Dress-up shoes. Sneakers. All neat and organized, in a row. Now, let's clean up this mess."

Mother begins to straighten the room. She hangs jackets back on hangers. The lamp is lifted to the night table. Kneeling, she reaches under the dust ruffle. "Oh, look! Your radio fell under the bed. Listen, you don't have to destroy your room looking for things. I'll help you find anything you need."

However, our girl does not wish to rely on her Mother. Not for everything. She crumples onto the floor, exhausted. "Ma?"

"What is it, sweetie?"

"Want my old life back. Can you help me find that?"

Mother's eyes fill. "Oh, Nellie."

She bends over to give her daughter a hug. "It'll get easier, you'll see. You're making so much progress. Look at how far you've come! Hang in there, sweetie. Okay?"

Nellie allows the hug briefly, then gets up and sits on the edge of her bed.

"What did you want your shoes for, anyway?" adds Mother, standing now. "It's getting late. It's not like we're going anywhere."

Well, maybe *you're* not, thinks Nellie.

"Right, honey?"

Nellie is not quite sure how to answer this. What she had planned to do was to practice gymnastics. She always *wants* to practice. Our girl thinks (mistakenly) that she has a meet next week. Maybe, *probably*, if not next week then definitely the week after.

But if she says she wants to practice to Mother, then Mother will say *no*, because Mother always says *no*—ever since the Accident. Or, even if she says *yes,* Mother will make Nellie wear that dumb helmet and only let her tumble—for like a second—on a fake mat on the grass. *So lame*, she thinks.

I was a champion! she wants to shout—to anyone who will listen.

Doesn't anyone remember?

So, therefore, Nellie must lie. Or rather, she makes a conscious decision to tell a lie, which in a way is progress, because in order to tell a lie, she must be able to discern fact from fiction, truth from untruth.

"So everything's okay now, sweetie?" Mother pats her head.

"Right, Ma. Not going anywhere. Going to bed, 'K?"

"This early?" Mother peers at her quizzically. "Don't you want to watch TV? I'll make us some popcorn. Dad's working, but Claire will be back soon. It'll be just us girls."

Nellie suddenly remembers she was looking for her Sister, too. "Where Claire go tonight?"

"She went to the movies. The five o'clock show. Don't worry. She'll be back soon. So how about that popcorn? What do you say?"

"No, Ma. Tired." Nellie shakes her head. "Very. Tired. Close door, please?"

Mother doesn't seem entirely convinced, but, resigned, she backs out of the room. "Okay, then. Goodnight. Sleep tight."

Nellie smiles at their old bedtime ritual. "Bedbugs bite."

"That's right, sweetie. You remembered."

After Mother closes the door, Nellie ambles over to the closet, the *correct* closet this time, and slips on her sneakers. She cannot actually tie them, but that's okay, she thinks, she does not need to.

She then begins wrapping her wrists with white athletic tape from her gym bag. One hand at a time. She makes an "L" with her left thumb and forefinger, which the lady at the rehab said can help her distinguish left from right.

I didn't become a champion overnight, Nellie is thinking. *And if no one in this family is going to support me, I'm taking matters into my own hands.*

(She cannot conceptualize this thought exactly—but that is the general idea.)

Unfortunately, *mes amis*, although I am in charge of most

things, it is clear that I am *not* in charge of our Nellie. The best I can do is watch as she finishes wrapping her hands, picks up her cane, and sneaks down the back staircase. Quietly, she slips open the screen door and heads outside, alone, into the night.

A FRIEND IS ALWAYS GOOD TO HAVE, BUT A LOVER'S KISS
IS BETTER THAN ANGELS RAINING DOWN ON ME.
—*Dave Matthews Band, Song # 40*

ADAM

When I stopped for gas, the quarter moon was a slice of orange peel in the sky. Now we're parked in front of Claire's house, the house I've only cruised by at least a dozen times.

It's been two weeks since we "kidnapped" her from the gym, but this is our first time out alone, without Sid or anybody else, *ever*. Hey, I'm still in shock that she said yes, and—get this— she actually reached for my hand in the movies. Now *that* was different and weird and progress . . . all at the same time.

It's a warm enough night to have the windows open. We can hear the sound of a TV from inside, which Claire says is probably her mom watching *Wheel of Fortune.*

"My dad's still at work. So we have to look out for his car, okay?"

Claire's already warned me not to call her house phone— ever—in case her pops should answer. But since my recent problems with the law, I'm not so crazy about having to sneak around.

"I'd rather just face him and get it over with, Claire."

172

"I know, but he's a control freak, okay? My mom knows we went out tonight. She's fine with it. I'll tell him eventually. He can't pick my friends forever, right?"

"No, I guess not," I reply, but I'm thinking, Are we only *just* friends?

The bedroom light is on upstairs, the one with the lace curtains. I wonder if her sister's up there hanging out. Alone?

"Would it help if Nellie came with us sometime?" I ask this 'cause I think it might impress her parents, but mostly 'cause I feel like such a lowlife scum for wanting to be with Claire instead.

"Maybe," she says, but then I see this look of hesitation fly across her face. This girl's so full of mixed messages that it's starting to screw with my head.

"Well, this music is nice," she says, resting her head against my shoulder.

"Yeah, thanks."

I've got a slow track playing now, Marley's "Stir It Up," which Cookie agrees, most girlfriends seem to like. I'd really like Claire to be my girlfriend. No doubt.

So, I put my hand on her knee and rub it gently. "Do you want to hang out tomorrow? Maybe as more than just friends?"

She nods. She seems good with that. In fact, she seems fine.

Then she's smiling this dazzling smile which is so much like Nellie's that it kind of hurts—but I still want to kiss her.

"Anyway," she says. "I guess I should go. Thanks again. I had fun."

"Yeah. Me too."

But before I even get a chance to make my move—

her back is to me, her hand is on the door handle, and the car door is opening, and she's about to slip away from me . . . *again.*

This is ridiculous—I've got to do something. "Claire?"

"What?"

"Just this." I pull her back and plant one on her. I can tell immediately that she wants it, too. Her lips feel warm and soft, and my hands wander around her neck and slim shoulders and get tangled up in her long, silky hair. She feels so, so incredible and then . . . and then . . .

And then she's not there anymore. I'm just sucking air.

What *the*—?

"Slow down," she says quietly, pushing me away. "Just stop, please."

So I make myself stop. *Not easy.* "Sorry. Did I do something wrong?"

"No, it's not you." Her hands fly up and cover her face. "This is so awkward. It's me."

Arghh. Not again.

"Fine, Claire. Whatever. All I ask is that you don't play games with me, okay? I understand if you don't want—"

"No," she interrupts. "I *do* want."

Huh?

Then she's touching my arm with her perfectly delicate hand. "There's just something I need to tell you first."

Sweet!

I try to act casual, like my curfew isn't in exactly thirteen minutes and I've only got eight more with her—that is, if I drive as fast as I can over the bridge, and—big *if* here—that cop isn't parked in his usual place tonight. Okay, maybe seven minutes. (Seven minutes of heaven. *He he.*)

Stretching my arms overhead, I slowly exhale. "I'm listening. Take as much time as you need."

"Okay. Well, do you remember when we were talking on the beach that night, and you were saying that Nick was so beneath me?"

I grin. "So true. How could I forget?"

"Right. Well, later on, when my sister and I were driving home, you know, after Nick beat you up . . ."

I slump down in the seat. "Did you *have* to mention that?"

"Sorry. Anyway, Nellie wanted to tell you that she loved you. It's the other reason why we were passing you that second time."

Could love actually happen that fast? I didn't feel anything like that for her sister—not then or especially now.

"Oh. I thought I heard her yell something."

"Right. But listen, there's more. When we were driving? After Nellie said that? I think it made me upset, because . . . well, okay, maybe I liked you, too. Somewhere deep down, I must have, right? Anyway, Nellie wanted to make sure there was nothing going on between us. It's one of the last things she said to me before the accident."

"Hmm." (I've found that saying *hmm* is useful when you have no clue what else to say.)

"I mean what if the accident didn't happen? My sister really liked you. You liked her, too, right?"

Okay, *enough.* Even if she thinks I'm an asshole for this, I've got to set the record straight.

"Listen. It wasn't going anywhere, Nellie and me. I'd already decided that on the beach, *before* the accident, okay?

I'm not sure why I liked her to begin with. Maybe it was to get closer to you. But let's say your sister was perfectly fine and the accident never happened, I'd still want you, okay?"

"Seriously?" She smiles. A relieved and (in my opinion) very sexy kind of smile. But then, like flipping a switch, she's upset again.

"But Nellie talks about it like you're still her boyfriend. What if she finds out about us? How will that make her feel?"

"We can deal with that, okay?"

She looks doubtful. "How?"

"Hmm."

"Seriously, Adam."

"Trust me. I'll figure something out."

Claire sighs and kind of folds her body into mine. "You know, I haven't exactly been the best sister to her. I'm really not such a good person."

"Yes, you are. Look, nobody's perfect. I know I'm not. But it's never too late to do the right thing, okay?"

"Sometimes it is," she whispers sadly.

"Well, maybe sometimes," I agree. "But not in this case. Your sister might be different now. But at least she didn't die."

Not like mine did.

Whoa! Where did *that* come from? I hardly ever let myself think about *that*.

"You're right," Claire says.

I'm not sure we've resolved anything, but then her face is so close to mine that I can't help it, I start kissing her again, and she kisses me back, and something spectacular is shooting through my entire body, and it's like neither one of us can stop. I don't want to stop kissing her . . . *ever*.

The night would have ended perfectly right there, but suddenly Claire is pushing me away again. She tilts her head like she's straining to listen.

Then I can hear it, too. A sort of whooping or yelling outside in the darkness. We peer out the car window. It sounds like it's coming from behind her house—or from the side yard.

"Oh, no!" Claire says with this panicked look on her face.

"What's wrong?"

"That's Nellie over there. Jumping on the trampoline. I mean, she could seriously get hurt!"

Claire bolts from the car, but I don't follow because when I look at the clock on the dash, it's five minutes before eight. I hate this freaking curfew! But I have no other choice—I have to fly home now.

"Sorry, I gotta go!" I shout. But Claire is running to get her sister off that thing, so I'm not sure she hears me.

Maybe it's fate, though, that I have to leave right at that second, because as I'm about to turn the corner at the end of her street, I look into my rearview mirror and I see Mr. Perry in his white van (with the "Perry's Sports" logo on the side) pulling into their driveway.

THE BRAIN IS WIDER THAN THE SKY,
FOR, PUT THEM SIDE BY SIDE,
THE ONE THE OTHER WILL INCLUDE
WITH EASE, AND YOU BESIDE.

THE BRAIN IS DEEPER THAN THE SEA,
FOR, HOLD THEM, BLUE TO BLUE,
THE ONE THE OTHER WILL ABSORB,
AS SPONGES, BUCKETS DO.
—*Emily Dickinson*

NELLIE'S BRAIN

"I hate you! I hate you! I hate you!"

From the trampoline, Nellie angrily watches the taillights of Adam's car drive away. *Bounce. Up. Down. Twist. Up. Down.*

Our girl is not accustomed to this emotion of anger. Everyone says she is different now, since the Accident, easily frustrated, harder to please, but she does not feel *that* different. Only when she cannot do something she was able to do before. Or when there is something she cannot remember no matter how hard she tries. Or when somebody tries to steal her boyfriend—*somebody* like Claire.

It was dark outside when Nellie left the house. She had trouble navigating the yard. She was about to go back inside when she saw that black car with the familiar license plates parked in front of her house.

Adam had finally come to visit her!

However, as you know, our poor girl was mistaken. When she peered into the car, there was somebody else sitting in the front seat with Adam. And they were so busy kissing that they did not even notice she was there.

Why would her Sister betray her this way?

Nellie ran over to the trampoline. She started bouncing. She is still bouncing. "I hate you, Claire! I hate you! I hate you!" she screams with every bounce. She does not care if she falls onto one of the poles. She thinks she would prefer that kind of pain.

But Claire is in the yard and she is shouting. "Oh, my god, Nellie. Get off. You're gonna get hurt!"

"No! Adam was my boyfriend. Mine! Mine! Mine! Mine!"

"I'm sorry! Let's talk about it. Stop bouncing, please!"

Nellie refuses to listen. *Who does Claire think she is*?

Suddenly the light over the garage snaps on, and Father appears in the driveway. "Get down from there, immediately, Nellie! Don't make me come up there and get you!"

The thought of her Father jumping on the trampoline makes Nellie smile to herself (just a little). "'K, sorry." She stops bouncing and sits down.

He is still angry as he turns to her Sister. "Why was she screaming at you, Claire? What did you do? Why weren't you watching out for her?"

Claire tries to explain. "I didn't even know she was out here, Dad."

Father is seething. "Both of you girls. Get inside. Now."

Later, when Nellie is in bed, Claire sneaks into Nellie's room. "I'm sorry," she says. "Please don't tell Dad that Adam was here." Nellie pulls a pillow over her head and pretends she is asleep.

After her Sister leaves, Nellie hears a noise outside. She gets out of bed and looks out the window. It is Father in the yard with a spotlight, disassembling the trampoline.

Remarkably, all is forgotten by morning. This morning our girl is excited. For once she is not being shipped off to rehab for the day—or stuck, bored to death, at home.

I am excited, too. We are planning to do something that is reminiscent of our old life: going on a road trip to the beach with friends. However, it almost did not happen. Mother was decidedly conflicted. "You can't let her out of your sight, Claire. Not after last night."

Nellie replied, "Not a baby."

But Claire was insistent. "Trust me," she pleaded. "Give me a chance."

And so Mother let them go.

It is a perfect, cloudless August day. And now Sid, Miles, Claire, and Nellie are walking along the beach, joking, laughing, and having fun.

"Look at cartwheels," says Nellie, pointing at the sand.

"What's she talking about?" asks Sid.

Along the river's edge, there are dozens of starfish that have washed up on the saltwater river's beach, swept in from the bay. This is a rare occurrence, but *quelle surprise!*

Spiny brown and pink appendages lie glistening in the sun.

"I get it," Claire explains. "You think the starfish look like they're turning cartwheels. Right, Nellie?"

"Right," she answers. Nellie thinks that Claire is one of the few people who truly understands her.

"No, they don't!" says Miles, scooping one up and sticking it in his red pail. "They're karate guys. Did you know I have a yellow belt now, Nellie?"

"'K." Nellie laughs. She bends over, leaning on her cane, and tosses another starfish into his bucket. "Here ya go, Miles."

The sand feels warm on Nellie's feet, even if it is tricky to walk with the cane. With her big toe she flips over a starfish, and the white suckers move like tiny worms. Two arms, two legs wide apart—they *do* look like cartwheels.

Nellie is wishing that she could turn a cartwheel, right *here*, right *now*, in the sand. Two months have passed since Nellie has cartwheeled. It is worse than when she injured her knee last fall. This time it feels like it might take forever to get back to the gym.

They will still not permit it, because of the Accident.

Our girl has little memory about the Accident itself. Only small glimmers— like bright lights, a loud thud—but that is all. Her Parents talk about it in whispers, and never to Nellie. Claire will not talk about it, either. (So many secrets in her family now.) They did not treat her this way before. She could practice anytime she wanted to. *Not until the doctors say you're ready, sweetheart.*

How is she supposed to *get* ready if she can't practice?

Her leg is feeling much better. On a whim, Nellie puts her cane down in the sand. Canes are for old people, she thinks. You cannot do a cartwheel with a cane!

Nellie holds her arms out, straight out like the starfish.

She hesitates. *How am I supposed to do this again?*

Then she remembers something Coach told her long ago. *Follow your fingers. Follow your fingers.* She reaches forward with her hands and throws her body down.

But her balance is off. Her elbows bend. She falls onto her shoulder and lies there, completely frustrated, and looks out to the water.

In the distance, on a rock in the river, are three long-necked seabirds called cormorants. They are sunning themselves with black wings extended, like shirts on a clothesline. They must dry their feathers first before they can fly.

"Nellie!" yells Miles, near the marshy grasses. "Get up. Come on!"

Nellie grabs her cane and hurries along, as best as she can. But when she reaches them and tries to join their conversation, she is quickly confused.

"How's that new girl doing at the gym?" Sid asks. "Tiny, right? Has she vaulted yet, Claire?"

Tiny, Nellie thinks. *Who's she?*

"No," Claire replies. "She's so stubborn. Just like you were, Sid. I can't seem to convince her."

Of what?

Sid laughs. "What was that silly thing Nellie used to yell right before she vaulted? Remember how she would get giant air?"

Nellie is thoroughly bewildered now. When more than one person is talking, it is hard to keep up. (*Mon dieu.* I wish it were easier, but it is not.)

Claire gives Sid a warning glance, like maybe Claire does not want her friend to talk about how Nellie was *before*.

"Don't go there, Sid."

"Where?" Nellie asks impatiently. "Tell me!"

"Okay. Just a minute." Claire sighs. "Could you ask her yourself, Sid? Just talk slowly. One word at a time."

Nellie listens carefully as Sid explains. "Remember, Nellie? When you would fly down the mat when you were little? Before you vaulted, what was that thing you used to say?"

Our girl thinks for a minute. "I know. Used to yell, Kow-a-bung-a." Nellie smiles because that memory is sweet.

"That's right," Sid replies, grinning. "How could I forget?"

All of a sudden, Nellie's eyes dart side to side, mischievously. And just like that, she heaves her cane near the water's edge and breaks into a tear down the beach. "*Kowabunga!*" she shouts, half-running, half-limping.

"No, Nellie, NO!" Claire yells, sounding frightened. "Stop! You'll get hurt!"

But there is no stopping our Nellie. She is charging and yelling and flying down the beach, when something shifts and connects and then explodes.

Nellie throws her hands down and then wondrously, her legs follow, pointed up, up, up, toward the sky. Her legs are not perfectly straight—how could they be?—but she did it. A cartwheel!

She did it!

We did it.

Fantastique!

Behind her, on the beach, Sid and Miles are cheering. "Yay! Nellie!"

"Are you all right?" yells Claire, worried. "Are you okay?"

Okay? Nellie is much more than okay. She is happy. Unbelievably fantastically, happy. She hugs her arms to her chest. That was *fun,* she thinks. *Mais oui.* So much fun! She cannot wait to do it again. And again and again.

Then she sees Claire marching toward her, pointing an accusing finger.

"Come back here, Nellie. You know you're not supposed to be running. Or doing cartwheels or anything. Not till your leg heals. Dad would be so mad."

Nellie is instantly remorseful. "Sorry, 'K? You're not tellin' him, right?"

Claire shakes her head. "Don't worry. I won't tell. But only if you promise not to say anything about Adam last night. It'll be our little secret, okay?"

Secret? Nellie nods. She remembers all about secrets. Claire promises to hold her secret tight. And she will keep her Sister's, too—at least for now.

WHAT I MEAN BY BAD THINGS, SID?
SECRET THINGS. THINGS NOBODY SHOULD HAVE TO DO. LIKE
PICKING UP DION'S BODY PARTS OFF THE SIDE OF THE ROAD.
SEARCHING FOR HIS BOOTS IN TWISTED METAL.
WE DON'T WANT THE JIHAD TAKING ANY TROPHYS.
YOU CAN'T UNDERSTAND, BECAUSE YOU'RE NOT HERE.
SO STOP TRYING SO HARD, OKAY?
—*Trey*

SID

When I get back from the Perrys' house, I run to the computer to see if there are any new e-mails for me. There's one from my dad, confirming his visit at the end of the month. He's bringing his new girlfriend, Tanya. He can't give me an exact day. But he hopes to spend some "quality" time with me. Him and Tanya, that is. Whatever, I'll see if I'm free.

Then, from the other side of the world, another e-mail pops up. This one's from Trey. And oh, my Lord, it's a bad one.

His best friend, Dion, is dead!

I start to type back an answer but then stop.

What does he mean about trying so hard to understand? Isn't that what good girlfriends do? How else am I supposed to comfort him?

Everyone's been warning me that Trey might be different when he finally comes back home. I didn't want to face it at first, but how could he *not* be different from that boy on the

Hawks football team, whose biggest bugout was when he thought he'd be benched for failing English?

That seems like such a long time ago.

I don't like to admit it, but it's hard to remember what it felt like when Trey kissed me or what he even *looks* like anymore, even though we went out for over four whole months before he left.

On the wall above my desk, I hung up all his best pictures: Prom last spring in his gray tuxedo, "bad-boy" pose on his front porch, cap and gown at graduation, so proud in his army hat and dress blues.

Suddenly, it hits me, really hits me: the next time it could be my boyfriend who's not coming back.

I take the last picture down and press my lips to his lips. *You told me once you were lucky, remember? Keep that luck going, for just a few more weeks, okay?*

I turn off my computer and go into the living room. It's almost nine-thirty. Miles is asleep, and my grandmother is watching a baseball game on TV. Coming from New Jersey, she's always up for seeing the Yankees beat the Sox.

She's also knitting a baby blanket for my cousin Destiny, who's expecting twins in September. I stand near the air conditioner, which is behind the TV, waiting for her to ask me what's wrong.

"That's A-Rod at bat now, baby. Could you move, please?"

I move to the other side, but I need her to listen to me.

"Why does everybody always leave me, Grams? Or have something bad happen to them? Or both?"

She looks away from the game. "What's going on, Sid?"

"Trey's best friend was just killed."

"Oh, no, that's terrible. What did he say?"

I tell her about his e-mail, then add, "I swear, sometimes I'm afraid Trey won't make it back alive—or when he does, we won't know each other anymore. I mean, Claire is still messed up from what happened to Nellie."

My grandmother motions me to lie down on the couch and puts her knitting aside. "Hard to say how he'll be. Sometimes bad things can make a person stronger. Families help. Trey got a good family? Like Claire's and Nellie's?"

For some reason my grandmother always compares everyone to the Perry family, like they're perfect or something. Maybe it's because Grams is raising us alone, or because they have a better house, better car, better things.

Okay, I used to compare myself to them, too. Like when Grams told me she couldn't afford gymnastics lessons anymore, I said that I wished I could live with the Perrys, which wasn't really one of the nicest things to say. But I don't feel that way now.

Of course I miss Claire's family the way it used to be, all laughing and cheerful and a place to get away from *my* worries. But it's not so cheerful anymore. Like tonight, when I was over there for dinner and Nellie was playing with her food, Mr. Perry hardly said two words to anyone—but he was especially mean to Claire. He said, "If you weren't running off all the time, your sister wouldn't have to resort to this to get our attention!" And after we had spent all day with Nellie!

Claire was so embarrassed. It was mad-awkward. I felt so bad.

"Yeah, Trey's got a good family," I tell my grandmother. "At least his mom and his sister, Latisha. But at the Perrys', things are so different now. I told you that Claire's been going out with Adam, right? But nobody's allowed to breathe a word to Mr. Perry—or he'll flip out. He blames all those kids from the party for what happened to Nellie. He's so bitter. I hate it."

I pause. "I mean both of them feel guilty enough already. Especially Claire."

"That's very sad." Grams motions for me to be quiet, as Jeter drives in a run. "Listen, time will help heal, Sid. Hopefully her father will stay strong and keep trying to love her."

That reminds me. "Yeah, just like my dad stayed strong for us, right? I hope he doesn't expect an invitation to my party. I mean, when he comes up here in a couple weeks, or should I say *if*?"

"Wait a minute." Grams gives me a sideways glance. "Your dad loves you, Sid. He's got his problems, is all. I'm sorry he's hurt you. But you know, when he was growing up, he was always causing trouble. Big trouble. I told myself I could probably deal with it if something bad happened to him—not that it wouldn't be hard, Lord, but somehow, it seemed much worse to think he might be responsible for somebody else's pain. Not much different from how Mr. Perry feels, I guess."

"What's your point, Grams?"

"Well, Jim Perry's not got it easy right now. That poor man's got both."

I realize she's right—and I wonder if Claire gets that.

"It's such a mess!" I punch the pillow on the couch. "I wish things could go back to the way they were before."

My grandmother takes my feet in her hands. "You got lots of stuff you're worrying about, Sidonia. Seems like you're getting sucked into other people's problems."

"They're my friends, Grams! What am I supposed to do?"

"Just remember, it's okay to worry about them, but you also need to take care of yourself. What are you doing nice for *you* these days?"

I think hard for a minute, trying to come up with something. "Well, I'm still having that party."

She gives me the eye. "You mean the party for Treyshawn?"

"Not only, it's for my birthday, too!"

"Okay, that's true enough," she says, laughing.

We had agreed to have the party on the beach at the end of our street. "Did you ask off from work yet?" I say.

"No, but I will. Seventeen years old, little girl. Where'd all that time go?"

I wonder where it went, too. My brother and I have spent the last seven of those years living in "kinship care" with my grandmother. I don't want to think about what we would do if anything ever happened to her.

She gets up off the couch. "It's hot. I'm thirsty. You want something to drink, Sid? Iced tea?"

"That sounds good," I say. But before she leaves the room, I reach over and wrap my arms around her waist, giving her a long, hard hug.

"What's that for?" she asks, smiling before she pulls away.

"That's for taking care of us, Grams."

THE GOAL OF THE WARM-UP IS TO RAISE THE BODY
TEMPERATURE. THE WARM-UP MAY TAKE AS LITTLE AS
10 MINUTES OR AS LONG AS AN HOUR! A GOOD SIGN THAT
THE WARM-UP HAS BEEN EFFECTIVE IS THAT
YOU ARE BREATHING HARD.
—*Make the Team*

CLAIRE

"I'm doing the best I can," I yell, leaning against Adam's car. I'm trying to stand up . . . *again*. The truth is, for a somewhat athletic person, I'm not so great at rollerblading—not compared to Adam, who's already circled back twice to see what's taking me so long. He told me blading is how he lost the weight. It's also helping him quit smoking, which he promised he'd do because I hate it.

For the record, I'm not such a fan of hot weather, either. If I were still with Nick, we'd be relaxing this afternoon in the air-conditioning, and I'd be watching him play video games. But Adam said he needed the exercise—I'm already sweating.

I take a step, then another, then, *oh, joy*, I fall on my butt before I even get two feet from his car.

"Are you okay, Claire?" He's barely suppressing a grin.

"Maybe. Define okay."

"You can do this," he says. "Try not to think." What I'm thinking is that he sounds just like my coach Melissa as he skates effortlessly in front of me.

I guess it's even more amusing (for *him*) when we finally get onto the bike path. I fall. Get up. Fall again. Soon I get stuck in the middle of this throng of kids on bikes. A little boy zooms past me, too close. The air billows his shirt out like a sail. For some reason, I grab hold of the end of his bike to steady myself, but suddenly, I lose my balance, my arms flail, and (I don't know how exactly) I slam into Adam—sending us both flying off the pavement onto the ground. The kid on the bike wobbles, then recovers, as he continues down the path.

"That was interesting," Adam says, rubbing his elbow as he sits up, wincing. "You didn't break anything, did you?"

"No. But I *told* you I wasn't good at stopping."

"Not true," he replies, tossing some grass at my head. "You absolutely *suck* at stopping."

And that's how it is with Adam. Even if I'm mad, I have to laugh. "Did you see the look on that kid's face?" I ask.

"He probably thought you wanted to steal his bike." We both start cracking up.

"Hey," he says, brushing off my shoulder. "Is it my imagination, or are you having fun?"

"Seriously. It's been so long since I've—"

"Shhh," he says, putting a finger to my lips. "I know."

He pulls me close, and he kisses me. Adam has this very gentle way of kissing. Usually, right before, he searches my eyes deeply, almost asking permission.

I think he's been a really nice boyfriend so far. Maybe the best I ever had.

So why then—and I hate myself for this—do I sometimes still miss being with Nick?

To distract myself from thinking about my ex, I begin nibbling at Adam's soft earlobe.

"Mmmm." He shivers and pulls away. "That's nice. But are you trying to get me in trouble?"

"I should probably come with a warning label," I admit, shrugging.

The bike path runs parallel to the beach. As we skate along, a dark cloud appears far off across the bay, and the entire sky quickly becomes overcast. Cold, fat, raindrops begin to fall, *plop-plop*, on my arm.

"Want to head back?" Adam suggests just as it starts to pour.

It's raining so hard that we have to huddle under this big oak tree. The downpour only lasts about ten minutes—but by that time we're drenched. I pull my damp shirt away from me, attempting to dry it. Adam shakes his dripping wet hair at me—back and forth like a dog. I guess he's trying to be funny.

"Stop it, you jerk! You're getting me wet!"

"Wet?" He squeezes out the excess water from the bottom of his shirt. "Don't you think the rain already did that?"

"Wet-*ter*," I say, smiling—then *not* smiling.

Because always in the back of my mind, like gathering storm clouds, are thoughts of Nellie. This time it's a memory from when we were younger. Another time I got drenched.

It was the summer right before I started high school, and I was working on my tan in our backyard. Nellie thought it would be funny to spray me with the garden hose. One minute I was lounging in the hammock, dreaming about my latest crush, and the next . . . freezing-cold water!

What the hell are you doing? I wrestled the hose from her, trapped her against the house, and blasted her—I didn't stop till she was crying and yelling for Mom.

Obviously, that's not the only time I've treated her badly. Just last Sunday when my dad was at work, Adam had the brilliant idea to bring her with us to a movie in the afternoon. Mom said okay, so I figured, why not?

It started out fun. Except that while we were waiting in line Nellie had to strike up conversations with all of these random strangers. Next she insisted on sitting between us— and kept trying to hold Adam's hand. Then, during the whole movie, she kept asking us to explain the plot to her. People were turning around and staring (she was ruining their entire movie experience), so I finally told her to shut up.

My exact words were, "Do you actually *want* people to notice that you're different?"

She looked crushed. But she copped an attitude, anyway. "Well, Adam doesn't think I'm diff'rent, right?"

He shook his head. "No. I think you're beautiful, Nellie." His eyes seemed to plead with me, *Be nice, Claire.*

"Love you, Adam," she said, purposely glaring at me.

When he went to get her more popcorn, I whispered, "He's not your boyfriend, Nellie. I've already told you that like three million times."

"He thinks I'm boo-ful, Claire."

Am I doomed to always be the bitch?

It's amazing, though: even after everything that's happened, she still gets all the attention, and she's *still* frigging annoying.

(The difference now is there's nowhere for me to put that feeling.)

I shake away those thoughts as the rain fizzles out to a slow, sprinkling mist. We decide to skate back to Adam's car and maybe go grab something to eat. Adam's ahead of me on the path, so I skate faster and reach for his hand. As he pulls me along, I close my eyes, and with the breeze in my hair, it almost feels like I'm flying.

You should have seen my sister. She could totally fly.

"Hey, Adam? Did you ever love somebody who drove you completely crazy at the same time?"

He gazes at me curiously. "Yeah, I think maybe I did."

I'm waiting for him to tell me who, but he keeps staring. At *me.*

Oh my god! Awkward. "I didn't mean . . ."

"Relax," he says, shaking his head. "I was thinking about my father."

Which makes me think about *my* father and how I lied to him about where I was going today, and how I made Adam pick me up at Sid's house, which is really not so nice for anyone—not Adam, not Sid . . . or my dad.

(Mom says I need to tell him about Adam soon, or she will. It's a miracle she's kept it from him all this time.)

We've made it back to the parking lot, and now I'm seriously crabby, which always happens when I think too much. Fish is waiting for me to take off my skates, and wouldn't you know it, the skates are giving me a hard time, too.

Finally, I get them off and throw them in the trunk. And that's when I notice, once again, his lame license plates: 4-CLAMS.

They're so old and rusted and, well, so corny. Before, when Adam was only my "friend," I didn't think I had any right to say anything. But now?

"Hey, did you ever think about getting rid of those, Adam?"

"Rid of what?"

"No offense, but . . ." I point at his bumper and make a face. "They kind of draw attention to you. In a not-so-very-cool sort of way. Remember when Nick and those guys almost ran you off the road?"

He doesn't answer. Just slams the trunk shut and gets into his side of the car. So I go around and get into mine. And we sit there. In silence. He's definitely pissed off. Maybe I went too far this time?

"Sorry. I won't bring up Nick anymore, okay?"

"It's not only that." His fingers go *tap-tap* on the steering wheel.

"What then?"

"I found those plates in our shed—right before I got my license. My dad held onto them all this time. They were from my mother's car."

"Oh." I feel kind of bad now. "Do they remind you of your mom? Is that why you're kind of attached?"

"Not really." His cheeks puff out with a long exhale, like he's been holding something in for a long time. "Before my mom left, I used to have a little sister. Her name was Molly, okay? So there were four of us. Four-clams, get it? But then she died."

I'm shocked. How could I be friends with him for so long and not know that? "Oh, I'm so sorry. I had no idea!"

"Yeah, well. It's not something I bring up casually in conversation. Besides, it was a long time ago. I was like seven years old. And she was little, only a baby. I don't remember much about her, except that her hands were tiny, like kitten paws. She used to hold onto my finger. Like this." He touches his index finger showing me.

I want to reach for his hand, but I'm afraid to move. To breathe.

"Things got really bad between my parents after it happened. Mom would deny it, I think, but that's the real reason she left. She couldn't forgive him, I guess."

"Why? Did your dad do something? What happened to Molly? I mean, *how* did she die?"

"My father was in charge of putting us to bed that night. Mom had taken her new car—he got it for her birthday, the day before—and she went out with some of her friends. Pop had a few beers, I guess, and when Mom got back, I was sleeping on the floor, and Pop was passed out on the couch.

"I remember waking up to screaming. It was a very scary scream. The police said it was accidental. They think it was SIDS. Sudden Infant Death Syndrome. Nobody knows exactly why it happens. But Mom swore she'd told my father to put Molly to sleep on her back—and he didn't. Maybe he thought he did, I don't know. But when I asked Mom, after everything, why they were getting a divorce, she said it was 'cause she couldn't trust him anymore."

Adam looks out the window so I can't see his face.

We trusted you, Claire. Obviously, we shouldn't have. None of it matters now, does it?

One night, one wrong decision, changes *everything*.

My heart is beating like mad. There's this awful pressure in my chest. I wait for as long as I can—then I have to ask. "But that was a long time ago. Does your dad still feel guilty about it? I mean, what does he say about it now?"

Adam turns to me angrily. "Now? I have no idea. We don't discuss it."

"*Never?* You never once brought it up?"

"Look, isn't it bad enough that he gets depressed every freaking summer? Talking would only make him feel worse."

Somehow, I don't think that's true. "Maybe. But it could also help. You never know."

Adam shakes his head. "You obviously don't know my father."

"You're right. But talking helped me. You and Sid. That night in your car. It didn't undo what I did—that part didn't change—but at least now I know that somebody sort of understands."

"Hey!" He nudges into me. "*Somebody? Sort of?*"

"I'm horrible. Sorry. I'll shut up now, okay?"

"No." He laughs. "I think you're perfect."

I frown. "Not even close."

The sun streams through the windshield, warming up his car. He turns on the ignition and rolls down the windows. "But." He hesitates. "There is this one thing you do once in a while . . ."

My stomach does a flip. "What? You *have* to tell me now!"

"Okay," he says, "maybe I shouldn't say this, but it kind of bothers me the way you treat Nellie sometimes. I know she drives you crazy and all, but, I mean, at least you still have a sister."

I can't even look at him after he says that. He's right. He's *so* right. When Nellie was perfect and normal, I couldn't handle it—and now that she's not, I can't take it, either. Will I ever be able to accept her exactly the way she is?

"God, I'm the worst sister ever," I tell him, meaning every word. "I really hate myself, Adam. Why do I have to be such a bitch all the time?"

"You're not," he says. "Well, not *all* of the time." He lets out a little laugh and smiles. "Ha-ha. Joking. You know that."

Without thinking, I punch him hard on his thigh. "Thanks a lot!"

"Why must you girls always hit me?" He rubs the spot then he smiles again. "Listen, if you really feel bad about how you treat Nellie, you can change that. You have time. Remember, it's never too late to—"

"Okay. I know." I shake my head. "I think somebody told me that once."

"Seriously?" He grins and pulls me into his arms. "Was it this geeky guy with uncool license plates who has this amazing crush on you?"

I can barely answer because my heart is in my throat.

"Yeah, do you know him?"

My heart is heavy to tell you this, but I'm not coming
home, Sid. My mom's upset. So's Latisha. They think I
should worry about getting my own self back. Worry
about my own family. But the people here are almost
more like my family now. Understand?
Be home in December, I think. Maybe.
If I don't re-up, again.
Like I told you before—you can't be waiting on me.
P.S. Be happy. Live your life.
And don't worry. I'll be fine.
—*Trey*

SID

"These are cute," says Claire, taking a package from off the
store shelf. The paper napkins have an *American Idol*
logo on them, blue and lime green silhouettes, with hands
holding microphones raised high in the air.

It's Sunday, late afternoon. We're at the Providence Place
Mall, picking out supplies for my party next weekend. *Those
napkins might be a nice touch for a ten-year-old's party, but
not mine.* "Are you serious?"

"I know. But you're really talented, Sid. Promise me you
won't bail next year. You can't keep putting your dreams on
hold. Not for anyone."

She's talking about this past April, when she offered to wait
in line with me in Cranston for the regional *Idol* auditions. She

knows the main reason I bailed wasn't because I didn't think I was good enough (although I'm probably not), but because of the one-in-a-million chance that if I *did* get a golden ticket, it might interfere with Trey's coming home. Not that I have to worry about that anymore.

"*Next* year?" I reply. "I was just hoping to get through today."

Claire touches my arm. "There are worse things that could've happened, Sid."

I huff and turn away. Like I don't know that? Sorry, but Trey's not coming home is one of the worst things that could have happened to *me*. Not to mention that he hasn't even contacted me since he dropped the bomb like a week ago. I'm completely devastated. Miserable. Sadder than sad.

"How 'bout this!" says Nellie, holding a feathered fake-diamond tiara to her head. "Could all wear them, Sid, 'K?"

"How about *not*," I snap, but instantly regret it.

"She's only trying to help," Claire replies, as if she's never been rude to her sister.

"I know, it's just that . . ." This is so crazy, I'm actually choking up again. Am I really going to have a mental breakdown right in the middle of Paper Party? I never wanted to be "that" girl, who falls apart over a boy, but hot tears are threatening to spill down my face. "I don't think I can handle it, Claire. I miss him so much."

"Oh, Sid, I'm sorry. It's so disappointing. Adam said to tell you he's sorry, too."

I want to believe her, but how sorry are my friends, really? I know they're all probably thinking I shouldn't waste another whole year on a long-distance romance. Grams keeps telling me I need to stop worrying about Trey and take care of myself.

Claire gives me a hug. "People can handle a lot more than they think they can, Sid."

"Okay," I say. But what if I can't? I mean *good for her* that she's all happy-happy again, now that she's seeing Adam—but here's the thing: I would've been with Trey in only *twelve more days*. Holding him, kissing him, feeling his strong arms wrapped around mine. We were almost there. I'd waited so long. Now it could be months.

(Or if something bad should happen to him—*never*.)

"What about these instead?" says Claire. I take the package from her, but when I look at the design, I get goose bumps. American flags, red, white, and blue—like a secret message from Trey.

Trey loves our flag. He says he's seen wounded men, chest-blown-open soldiers, taking their last breath from a stretcher and saluting the flag. Trey told me the flag is what they're fighting for, or at least what our flag represents.

I guess that's true, and I'm the first one to believe in freedom—but does all that freedom have to come at such a high price? And why do my boyfriend and I have to be the ones to pay it?

"Do you think it's selfish, Claire? Throwing a party when people are dying thousands of miles away?"

"It's your *birthday*, Sid."

"Not just mine. Did I ever tell you that Trey and I were born exactly three years apart?"

"Maybe once or twice?" Claire laughs. "You're always

putting everyone else first. Even Adam says so. You should definitely have the party. You deserve to have some fun."

She's right, except that she hasn't exactly been specializing in the "fun" department lately. "Like you're one to talk!"

"I'm trying," she says sadly. "I'm here with you now, right?"

"I know. I just miss the way things were before."

"We'll hang out more, I promise." Then her eyes get excited like back in the day, when either of us would come up with some crazy plan.

"What if we put together a care package for the troops, Sid? Didn't Trey say they needed shaving cream and wipes and things like that? If you asked everyone to bring something, you'd have an instant, guilt-free party."

She's right. It's a great idea!

But I'm still not sure about those flag plates. They make me uneasy.

Nellie picks up a different package. "I like pink," she says, pointing. "You get these Sid, 'K?"

Nellie looks sweet today, with her cute new bob and blonder highlights. Even if she is wearing this crazy mix of clothing: a long brown velvety skirt with a short-sleeved white top, and her beige winter Uggs.

"Let me see those." Claire looks at them, smiles, and then hands them to me. "What do you think?"

Peace signs, hot pink and black. Out of all the things we've looked at, I like these the best. I'm hesitating, though. "Are you sure they're okay? I wouldn't want to seem disrespectful to the troops."

"But isn't peace what Trey's fighting *for*? I think they're perfect."

⁓

After I pay for my stuff, we go out into the mall again. Nellie is begging for a Dell's lemonade and hot pretzel, so we take the escalators to the food court. There are floor-to-ceiling windows on the third floor that overlook the city. Trey's family lives only a few blocks from here. I wonder if we have time to stop in and say hello—I haven't seen his sister, Latisha, in almost a year.

But Claire wants to meet up with Adam later, and he has that curfew thing—so there probably won't be time. For taking care of my needs, I mean.

What else is new?

We're standing outside Sam's Music Store when Claire says she has to do one more errand. "Do you mind, Sid? I'm going to run in here for just a sec." She adds that we shouldn't come in after her, *hint, hint.*

So I guess my birthday present won't be a total surprise.

In the meantime, Nellie's chewing on her hot pretzel. "I'm cole," she complains, taking a slurp of her lemonade. "Forgot our coats, Sid."

It's always freezing cold in this mall in the summer, with the AC and all. To distract her, we sit on a bench in front of the store, and I point out which boys I think are cute. Actually, I'm purposely pointing out the ones who aren't—and she thinks that's so funny. She's laughing too loud, but who cares?

"That one look like Adam," Nellie says, staring at a kid with brown hair.

Despite all of Claire's attempts to talk Nellie out of it, apparently she is still stuck on him. "Adam gonna be at party, Sid?"

"Yeah. But so will lots of other boys, Nellie. You'll see."

Suddenly excited, she tugs on my sleeve and points to some people coming out of the American Eagle store across the way. "Know them, Sid. Right? What's her name again?"

Crap! It's Meredith. She's with Kristen and Gabby, who are wearing short-shorts and halter tops with high platform sandals. Mall prowl wear.

"Want to say hello," Nellie announces, starting toward them.

I grab her arm. "No, I don't think so. Your sister doesn't like—"

"Hey, you!" Nellie yells anyway, waving. "Over here!"

I shoot her a glare. "Didn't you hear me, Nellie?"

"*Know* them, Sid."

When they see us, they wave back and begin walking over. They each have a pink shopping bag from Victoria's Secret tucked under their arms.

Claire, who's just come out of the store, isn't exactly pumped to see them, either. "Oh, joy."

I nod. "Seriously. Blame your sister."

When they get here, Nellie stands overly close to Meredith. I've noticed she doesn't exactly get the whole "personal space" thing since the accident. She pets Meredith's shopping bag like it's a cat. "I like your pink. It's shiny."

"Nellie, don't," says Claire, pulling on her arm.

Meredith steps back and side-glances at Kristen.

"How's your summer been, girls?" I say, trying to move the conversation off of Nellie.

"Great, great," says Gabby. "Lots of fun."

"My summer's great, too," says Nellie, piping in.

After a second, Kristen shifts her shopping bag onto her other shoulder. "We heard about you and Fish, Claire. But that's just a lame rumor, right?"

"No," says Claire, defensively.

"No, you *are* going out?" Meredith asks. "Or no, it's a lame rumor?"

When Claire doesn't elaborate, Meredith shrugs. "Oh, well, anyway, as I'm sure you know, Nicky's about ready to go off to college. On Labor Day. He wants me to help move him in." She glances down and readjusts her orange halter over her tiny boobs, smiling smugly.

Even though my best friend and I have gone over the million reasons why she was right to break up with Creep-o, Claire's upset to hear this, I can tell.

Then, to show off, I guess, Gabby pulls a red Juicy Couture jacket from another bag and slips it on. "Why do they keep it so freezing in here? What are you girls shopping for, anyway? School stuff?"

"No," Nellie replies. "Sid's havin' party."

Meredith is instantly all over that. "A party, Sid? When?"

Of course I was going to be evasive, but then Nellie pipes in again. "Tomorrow! Or next week. Right, Sid?"

"It's not really a party," I explain. "Just a few people. We've decided to collect things to send over to the troops. You know."

"What?" Meredith pretends like she's crushed. "And you weren't going to invite us, Siddy? We'd *love* to come to your party. What should we bring? What *time*?"

Claire shoots me a warning glance, but I figure Meredith probably won't show up (or won't stay long if she does), so I tell her it's at our beach on the river, next Saturday, at five.

Finally, after all of that, I'm thinking we can make our escape—but no.

Out of nowhere, Nellie blurts out, "Mer'dith! That's your name, right?" She elbows me in the ribs. "Told you I knew her, Sid."

There's a beat when nobody says a thing. Poor Claire looks like she wants to sink into the beige marble floor and disappear.

Meredith replies, "Of course you *know* us, Nellie." She pronounces each word super-slow. "We're. Your. Sister's. *Friends*."

I don't think Nellie understands that Meredith isn't talking this way to be nice or kind. "Come on, Nellie," I say. "Let's go."

"No," Nellie insists. "No! Want to stay!"

Meredith leans toward me and whispers, "Will she always be this limited, Sid?"

I'm so mad I want to scream!

Claire pulls on Nellie's arm. "Come on, Nellie. Please? Mom's going to worry if we're late."

But Nellie refuses to budge. Instead she stares at Meredith. "I make you uncomf-table, right?"

"Um, no," Meredith replies nervously. "What do you mean?"

"Well, somebody should told you. I have this problem with C.R.S."

"C.R.S?" Meredith repeats at me, like I should translate. But when I glance over at Claire, she doesn't seem to know what Nellie's talking about, either.

"Kid said at rehab," Nellie explains. "It means, 'Can't remember shit.' Get it, Mer'dith? C.R.S? Can't remember shit? That's me!" Then she slaps Meredith hard on the back and laughs and laughs.

I can't believe it. Amazingly, Nellie has *totally* called her out, and what's even better is Meredith's mortified expression.

I shake my head, laughing. "You're way *too* funny, Nellie."

Claire puts an arm around her shoulder. "That was awesome."

But Meredith can't stop herself from spazzing. She practically stomps her sandaled foot in frustration. "Well, I don't understand what's so funny. I mean, do you really think you should be laughing at her, Sid?"

Claire grabs for Nellie's hand, protectively.

"But we're not laughing at *her*, Meredith," I say, smiling. "Sorry. You're probably just too *limited* to figure that out."

CLAIRE

There's no limit to what these girls can pack into their gym bags: water bottles, hand grips, beam shoes, iPods, magazines, stuffed animals—somebody even brought their pet hamster once! They're getting ready to leave for the afternoon.

"Don't forget, girls!" Melissa shouts. "Only four more days!"

It's the last week of camp. The last week of summer. On Labor Day we're having an exhibition meet against the Yellow Jackets, our rivals. We were in decent shape, too, until this afternoon when Samantha twisted her ankle coming off the beam. We've never lost to this club in our pre-season opener before (an ego thing for Melissa), but now with Sam limping around, things aren't looking so good.

Which brings us to Tiny.

Actually, Tiny has made *some* progress. She's doing okay on floor. But her bars are a disaster, and she still hasn't gotten up the courage to vault. She absolutely refuses to go near it. I think she's working as hard as she can, but Melissa disagrees.

She's got this thing about conquering your fears in order to achieve your personal best.

Try and fail, girls. But don't fail to try.

Melissa actually said to me this afternoon, "Do whatever it takes." Meaning to get Tiny to vault. "We're going to need every point now, Claire."

What else am I supposed to do? The girls' rides will be here in a few minutes, so there isn't any time left today, but then I get this brainstorm while we're sitting on the mat waiting. I decide to tell Tiny about what happened to my sister—the accident, her brain injury, everything—hoping it might inspire her. For once, she seems to hang on my every word.

"Anyway," I add at the end, "it could be sort of like you're vaulting for Nellie—'cause she can't. Did I tell you she's coming next Monday to watch you compete?"

"For real?" Her eyes get very wide. "But can you get hurt that bad from just hitting your head?"

(Leave it to her to zero in on the hurt factor.)

"Well, yeah. But remember, Nellie wasn't wearing a seat belt. You've seen the other girls vaulting all summer. We have that nice soft mat behind you. It's really safe."

"Okay. Let's do it." She gets up off the floor.

What? I'm amazed. "You mean *now*?"

"It's for Nellie, right?" She slips off her sneakers and sticks her hands in the chalk bucket. "Will you spot me, Miss Claire?"

Before she changes her mind, I hurry over and stand next to the vault. Immediately, Melissa realizes what's going on and motions for Samantha (who hasn't left yet) to come and root for her.

Using Jenny for a crutch, Sam hops over and begins to clap. She elbows Jenny to cheer, too. "Push it, Tiny! Go, girl! Go!"

Tiny stands at the far end of the gym, wringing her hands. As we watch, she runs toward me, gradually gaining speed.

"Come on!" I yell. "You can do it! Do it for Nellie!"

She's almost here. I can't believe it. Who would have thought it could be this easy? But then . . . before she reaches the end of the runway . . . she *closes her eyes.*

Who closes their eyes in the middle of running?

It's hard to look at, like a train wreck about to happen, but I watch as her eyes suddenly fly open and she stutter-steps off to the side. I hear Samantha mumble, "Good try." Melissa just shakes her head.

When I try to approach her, Tiny won't even look at me. She glumly stares at the wooden floor. "I suck, okay? Don't tell your sister."

The poor kid. I put my arm around her shoulders. "Hey, my sister would be proud of you. You tried, right? And this isn't about Nellie, it's about *you.* You got really close that time. It was awesome. I honestly think you can do it. But you've got to decide. Do you want to learn how to do this—or not?"

She nods. "I think so."

"Okay. Listen, I have an idea. Can you get to the gym extra early for the rest of the week? Around seven o'clock?"

"That early? Maybe. I could ask my mom."

"Well, if you can, we'll just do vault. You and me. All day long. For the next four days, till you get it. We're going to get you flying!"

"You think?" She grins her silly, big, toothy grin. "We'll make Nellie so proud."

"And we'll make *you* proud, too. But you've got to promise to keep your eyes open next time."

"I *did*," she argues until I glare at her. "Maybe not the whole time," she admits, shrugging.

(It might be a very long four days.)

A few minutes later, Tiny's mother arrives to pick her up. Surprisingly, she gives me some really nice compliments about how much I've helped her daughter. And she agrees to bring Tiny in early tomorrow and the rest of the week—so we definitely have a plan.

After they go, I realize I'm feeling genuinely happy all of a sudden. The happiest I've felt in a while. In fact, I'm feeling so good, I think I might just stay for a bit and practice. I let Melissa know.

I've been working with Melissa for half the summer on a back handspring—on beam. It's a move that most gymnasts (like Nellie) master at a much younger age. But for some reason, I've always had this mental block. In the past, I would just stand there for an eternity until someone would yell, "Get off, already!"

Can you blame me?

A back handspring is one of the most dangerous moves you can do on beam. One misplaced step? But I can't think about that, because if you miss it . . . well, let's just say you *can't* miss it.

Melissa told me to use my visualizations. *Picture it in your head, Claire. Imagine that you've already done it. Your body will know what to do.*

When I announce that I'm finally ready, Melissa comes over to spot me. "I can do this," I tell her.

"It's not me you need to convince," she replies.

She's right.

I stand in the middle of the beam with my back facing the direction I want to flip. My heart thumps with the sudden rush of adrenaline. Nellie's voice is in my head: *Now! Do it now, Claire. Before you change your mind.*

I start to jump, arching backward behind me. My hips thrust forward, and I push my shoulders behind—just as my feet leave the beam. Toes pointed, legs pressed together. Now for the fun/scary/dangerous part, as my body flips over, I grab the beam with both hands and push away. My legs fly over, and my feet land right on target.

All this happens in seconds—then it's over.

I stand there, amazed, staring at Melissa. "Oh my god! I did it. I actually didn't fall."

"You nailed it. That was great!"

I hop off. "Well, it's a lot easier if you keep your eyes open."

Melissa laughs. "Can you believe Tiny did that before? She turned out to be a sweet kid, though."

"She just needs more confidence. Like I did, I suppose. When I was competing way back then."

"Way back in April, huh?"

Was it only last spring? It seems like much longer.

Melissa eyes me gently. "Actually, you've always had lots of potential, Claire. But if somebody could throw a trick better than you, you just kind of gave up. If you hadn't . . . I mean, who knows? You might have been . . ."

"What? I was never in the same league as you—or my sister! And you know it."

"Maybe not. But your sister never gave up. Talent,

perseverance, passion. That's a three-punch combination—extremely hard to beat." She gazes off in the distance as if remembering a time when there wasn't anyone that she or my sister couldn't beat.

In my gym bag, my cell phone is ringing. We both glance at it, but I don't pick up. Melissa looks apologetic. "I didn't mean to compare you."

"That's okay. I'm used to it."

Melissa frowns. She seems kind of nervous. "How is Nellie since she's come home, Claire? I usually don't ask, because, well, it seems hard for you to talk about."

"It is. But I don't mind telling you." I clear my throat. "Nellie's okay. Different. Funny—she cracks us up. But she forgets a lot, too. She's got this problem with short-term memory loss. A big problem."

My coach stares uncomfortably at her whistle, like maybe she's sorry she asked.

I shrug. "Of course, she wants to start gymnastics again. The doctors are against it—even if she wears a helmet, there's a risk. But I don't think my parents can put her off much longer."

"Really?" she says, smiling. "It would be *wonderful* to have her back here."

As I watch Melissa's face brighten, I'm worried about getting her hopes up too high. "But my sister might not ever be any good again—you realize that, right?"

Melissa moves toward me. "I'm really sorry," she says, twisting the cord for her whistle again. "This must be so hard for you, Claire."

For *me?* The more time that goes by, the more I realize how hard it is for *everyone* who loves my sister.

"Right. Well, you probably miss coaching her, huh?"

She hesitates, as if wanting to protect me, but then her voice catches. "To be honest, I miss your sister just about every time I walk in here."

It's too much. I can't help it. I start to cry.

Awkwardly we come together, and Melissa hugs me. We stand there rocking for a few minutes—until I pull away. "So, anyway, school's starting next week," I say. A pathetic attempt to change the subject.

"Only one season left. I can't believe you'll be graduating this year."

"Along with half the team." I think of Sara, Julia, and the rest of the girls; I can see them in my mind, getting ready for a meet. It's what they all live for.

Melissa looks serious. "While we're on the subject, have you thought about competing again? I know you said you were here just to practice, Claire, but the team sure could use you."

Do I want to put myself through that again?

"Maybe. I mean, I know I've improved. But if there was someone else as a backup to take my place?—I wouldn't want you guys to lose because of me."

She frowns. "After all these years, I hope you know that this gym is about more than winning, Claire."

"I know," I reply. But I wonder how my dad would feel, seeing me out on the floor instead of my sister. And despite what Melissa says, I know she might be wishing Nellie was out there, too.

So many people's dreams were wrapped up in my sister's success. Why did this have to happen to us?

When Melissa shuts off the lights, the humming of the big overhead fans slows and then stops. I walk toward the door, but I don't want to leave yet. I know it might be hard for her to answer, but there's one more thing I have to ask.

"Melissa? I've been wondering. When you first heard about the accident, did you ever wish it was *me*, you know, who got hurt—instead of Nellie? I'd understand if you did. I mean, she was destined for—"

"Absolutely not!" She looks truly upset by my question. "Not once. Never, Claire. I only wished . . ." She pauses.

"What?"

"I wished it didn't happen at all."

NELLIE'S BRAIN

"Party. Party. Party. Party!" Nellie exclaims. "Today, right, Claire? Right?"

Our girl is exuberant; she is jumping on Claire's bed she is so excited. She has brought in an armful of clothing from her closet, which she dumps in a mound on top of the fluffy blue comforter.

Her Sister dives under the sheets. "Get out of here, Nellie!"

I could have predicted that Claire was not going to appreciate all that clamoring, especially not so early on a Saturday morning, but *you* try communicating that to Nellie.

Status update: Many of our girl's basic skills have returned. I am pleased to report that we do not have to tax ourselves as strenuously, for example, to cut up food, or read, or brush our teeth.

Also, I am becoming accustomed to our limitations. Frustration, for the most part, has been replaced by acceptance. *D'accord,* it is a good feeling, this integration, this working together as a team.

But back in bed, trying to ignore her, Claire cradles a pillow over her head.

"You're making me so mad," she says with clenched teeth.

"Sorry. Time to,"—Nellie lunges and pulls the pillow away—"wake up! Think should wear this? Or this? Like this top, 'cause it's shiny. Do you?"

Claire opens her eyes. "If you don't get out of here right now, it won't matter how damn shiny your top is! I'll throw it out the window! And go to Sid's party without you!"

"What?" Nellie takes a minute to register this information. "No, you won't! I'm telling. MAAAAAAAAAAA!!!!"

A few seconds later, Mother peeks into the room. "What's going on?" She is wearing her yoga clothes, blue tights with a long T-shirt. She looks rested and calm. "Leave your sister alone, Nellie. Come downstairs so she can sleep."

"No, wait." Claire sits upright in her bed and stretches her arms over her head. "It's okay, Mom. I'm awake now, sort of. Let me see one of those, Nellie."

Nellie selects a purple shirt with white butterflies down the sleeves and hands it to her Sister.

"Oh, that's cute. But I just got something that might look even better. It's in that bag by my closet. Go get it and see."

Nellie scrambles across the bed, finds the bag, and takes out a soft pink halter top. As she holds it up, a wistful glance passes between Claire and Mother. Maybe they are thinking how much different this Nellie is from the one before. Or perhaps they are hoping that the worst is now behind them.

Alors, I wish that I could reassure them.

"You can borrow that tonight if you want, Nellie."

Mother mouths the words, "Thank you." She smiles proudly at Claire and backs out of the room. "Just call down if you need me, girls."

The sun is bright through the white blinds of the bedroom window. Patiently, Claire watches as Nellie tries on ten different outfits and spins around in each one. "Think Adam like this one? Or this better?"

Her Sister frowns. "I thought you were okay with us being together, Nellie. Don't you remember? He talked to you—"

"I know!" Nellie says with a grin. "Just kidding. Getting my *own* boyfriend tonight."

Stepping around her, Claire shakes her head skeptically. "Oh, really?"

"I am! You'll see."

"Whatever, Nellie." Claire grabs a towel from the hook on her door and announces that she is going to take a shower. But as she passes Nellie, she makes a point to sniff at her Sister's hair.

"Well, I hope you smell better then you do right now—or no boy will want to come near you!"

Nellie can tell that her eyes are teasing. Nellie laughs. "Ha-ha. Not funny!" When she stops laughing, she notices that her stomach has begun to rumble.

"'K. Have nice shower. I'm hungry now."

Nellie leaves Claire's bedroom and runs her finger along the flowered wallpaper as she sashays down the hall. From the top of the stairs she can smell something cooking. A good smell is coming from the kitchen. The staircase is steep. *Careful. Be careful*, is what Mother has told her.

She puts her hand on the railing. Halfway down, Nellie has to stop and think, *Which way is the kitchen?* Sometimes she can get confused in her own house. *Left or right at the bottom of the stairs?*

Left, she decides. But before she turns the corner, she overhears her Parents talking, so she waits. Nellie has found that People will say interesting things—secret things—when they think you are not there.

It is unusual for Father to be in the kitchen on a Saturday morning. He is taking time off from Perry's Sports for a "mini-vacation." Nellie hears Mother ask if he needs anything while she is out. He says no, but then he reminds her about his Sister Lucy's picnic, this afternoon.

"The girls are coming with us, right, Nancy? You know Ray is always asking about Nellie."

"Oh, right," Mother answers. "But they have this party later. We can't stay too long."

"*Party?* What party?" Father sounds irritated.

"Didn't I tell you? Sid's birthday. Listen, I'm out the door to yoga, Jim. We'll discuss it when I get back, okay?"

After the door shuts, Nellie goes into the kitchen.

"Good morning, sweetie." Father stands near the stove, cooking breakfast. He is wearing his plaid slippers and blue bathrobe.

"Hi-ya, Dad." She peers around his wide shoulders and watches as he flips something round and brown in the frying pan. It looks good and tasty, but what is it?

Our girl does not want Father to know that she is having trouble remembering the word for what he is making. He always gets this funny look on his face whenever she cannot remember something, like it is disappointing *him.*

Only a dumb word, she thinks whenever that happens. *What's the big deal?* She is getting used to not having the right word all of the time. Yet, a part of her wants to please him; it has always been that way.

"Smells good, Dad." She is hoping to trick him into telling her what "it" is.

"Thanks, Nellie."

"Can I have some those . . . ?"

Not cupcakes, right?

"Sure, honey. I'm making enough for everybody."

Merde. He is definitely not helping.

Think, Nellie, *think. Réfléchis.*

As Father sifts powdered sugar over the finished stack, Nellie goes to sit on the stool at the counter. At least she remembers that they are called a *stack* of something, anyway.

Sandy jumps up into Nellie's lap, startling her. Since the Accident, there are times when things seem to appear out of nowhere: People, conversations, cats. Gentle paws knead her leg, and Nellie puts her nose into Sandy's fur. *Soft. Warm. Love.* Nellie does not have to worry about finding the right words for Sandy.

Just then, Claire comes into the kitchen. Her long wet hair grazes Nellie's arm as she passes. "Those pancakes look great, Dad," she says, opening the refrigerator door.

"*Pancakes!*" shouts Nellie.

Father looks upset. "You forgot the name for them, didn't you?"

"No, she didn't," Claire says, pouring herself a glass of orange juice. "You love pancakes, right, Nellie?"

Nellie nods. She used to love pancakes slathered with butter and maple syrup—but not anymore.

"Here, sweetie." Father puts a plateful in front of her

on the counter, along with a knife and fork.

"Where's ketchup, Dad?" Nellie eats everything with ketchup now, something she never used to do . . . *before*.

Claire hands her the bottle from the shelf in the refrigerator. When Nellie turns the ketchup upside down, it squirts out with a loud noise like farting.

"Gross, Nellie." Claire makes a face. "That's soooo disgusting!"

Father scowls; he is getting upset. Nellie has noticed that although Mother is not as sad anymore, and Claire is much nicer, Father will often wear his angry face or disappointed eyes. "Don't make fun of her, Claire."

Anxiously, Claire looks over at Nellie. "She knows it's gross, Dad. I kid her all the time. Right, Nellie?"

Nellie smiles at him. "It's 'K, Dad. Think's funny."

"Well, I don't." Father returns to the stove again. (If you want my opinion, for someone on a minivacation, he does not seem very relaxed.) "So, what's this your mother told me about a party tonight, Claire?"

Nellie knows—right away—this is what he is actually upset about.

Claire takes a sip of orange juice. "Sid's having a birthday party. She invited Nellie and me. We're supposed to help set up."

With that, Nellie gets that excited feeling again from this morning. She has not been to a party in ages. At least not since . . .

Did you ever do a Jell-O shot, Claire? No? They're yummy.

Nellie has begun to have glimpses of what happened that night. She is still not quite able to put it all together—it is more like one of those big jigsaw puzzles they have at the Rehab Center. Or the *Where's Waldo?* book they make her search through every day. (She can never seem to find that guy!)

Maybe at first she was afraid of knowing the details, but not anymore. Our girl can handle a lot more than they think she can. In fact, Nellie would have asked Claire about the crash the other day at the mall, but then they ran into—*What is her name again?*—and Claire has been very busy lately with Adam.

At least Nellie understands now about Adam. He explained that Nellie will always have a place in his heart, but he does not love her, not like she deserves.

Passion is something you can't talk yourself into, he told her. *It just is.* Nellie smiled and agreed. She has always had a passion for gymnastics. No one had better try to talk her out of that!

"Adam's comin' to the party," Nellie blurts out, then covers her face, as if she has said the wrong thing. She peeks out at Claire.

Father scowls and raises his eyebrows. *"Adam?"*

"He's nice," Nellie explains. "I liked him. Claire's boyfriend now."

"Adam *Silva?*" Dad says, louder, interrupting. "Since when is he *your* boyfriend, Claire?"

Claire shoots Nellie a please-shut-up-now glance. "Calm down, Dad. We've only seen each other a couple times. Nothing serious."

"I hope not! That really disappoints me, Claire. But, I'm curious. What makes you think I'm going to let you go to a party? With a boy who brought a keg to the last one? Do you think I'm some kind of idiot?"

Claire is pouring syrup over her pancakes. Pouring, pouring.

"Well, do you?" he repeats, slamming the silverware drawer.

"Adam doesn't drink, Dad. And stop acting like he's some random guy. He made that one mistake, but he's paying for it, okay? Besides, I can't ask Sid to un-invite him! It's *her* party. Sid would be crushed if we didn't go. Pearl will be there supervising. And Mom already said it was okay. So, don't worry. We'll be fine."

Father brings the pan over to the sink. When he turns on the faucet, there is a hissing cloud of steam. "Well, it might be fine with your mother, but what if it's not fine with me? I mean, Sid's grandmother? On her own, with a bunch of rowdy teenagers? And who will be watching your sister while you're off doing whatever with *keg*-boy?"

"Dad, please don't call him that! We promised Sid—"

Nellie is upset now. "Not baby, Dad. Can take care of self!"

"I said no, Claire. I mean it!" He turns to Nellie. "Forget about it, honey. I don't feel comfortable about this."

Abruptly, Claire pushes her stool away from the counter. "Why don't you just come out and say it? This has nothing to do with Adam or Sid's grandmother. Or the party. You don't trust me anymore! And you never will!"

"What? That's simply not true—"

"Yes, it is. You think you're the only one who's suffering? It wasn't *your* fault, Dad. *I'm* the one who has to live with what I did! Every single day. For the rest of my whole frigging life!"

Claire runs out of the room and up the stairs. A door slams. Something falls to the floor. *Mon dieu.* Since the Accident, it is confusing for Nellie when people fight or yell. Their voices are jumbled and their emotions are hard to read, but our girl knows what this fight was about.

When Father scrubs at the pan, a lemony scent from the dishwashing liquid fills the room—but it doesn't take away the smell of disappointment.

"Not nice to Claire, Dad."

"No, I guess not." He wipes his hand on a dish towel. "Your sister thinks I blame her for what happened. Maybe I did at first, but I don't anymore. You don't realize how vulnerable you are, Nellie. I don't want anything to happen to you. To either one of you girls."

He clears his throat and looks away. "I couldn't take it. Not ever again."

Suddenly, Nellie feels sad for her Father. But despite what he claims, Nellie is thinking that maybe he does still blame Claire, *just a little*. She has seen how his mouth twitches downward when her Sister comes into the room. He does not want to blame her, but he does.

Nellie is thinking perhaps she can change that, *juste un peu*.

"I drank shots at party, Dad. Did Claire tell you that? My choice. *Me.* She told me slow down, but didn't listen. She tell you that?"

"What?" He drops the towel. "What are you saying?" Father runs his hand over the back of his neck.

"I told her pass Adam's car!"

224

He looks shocked. "You did? I just assumed that she . . . that you . . . well, no, I guess Claire didn't tell us that part. No."

He seems old and tired. *Vieil homme fatigué.*

Has she worn him out? He seems worried, too.

Nellie wonders, *Is he always going to worry like this?*

She wants to reassure him. She thinks for a minute, trying to figure out the right thing to say. Finally, she has it. "Wanna be normal, Dad. Wanna do normal things. Don't you want me have any fun?"

"Normal? What's normal?" He gazes is out the kitchen window to the side yard. A circle of brown grass marks where the trampoline used to be. He smiles sadly. "Yes, of course I do."

"Then let me go Sid's party! *Please?* Claire will watch out for me. She did already at movies. At mall. On beach. Always does."

He scratches at his unshaven face. "I don't know. I'm just not sure. Your mother thinks it might be okay?"

Nellie senses that Father is changing his mind. Out of everyone in the family, she has always been able to read him best. She walks across the room and gives him a hug. A hug will make him feel better; it always does.

He squeezes her hard in return. "It's only because I love you, Nellie."

"I know. Love you, too, Dad." She tiptoes up and kisses his cheek. "But can't protect me for rest of life. Know you want to, but can't. Nobody can, 'K?"

"Okay, Nellie. You win." He smiles, but there is a painful resignation in his eyes.

Ah, *mes amis*, you may not know this yet, but this is the most heart-wrenching paradox of being a Parent: they do not want you to come to any harm, but know that they must let you go.

SID

4:15 P.M. A strong, steady breeze begins to blow through the trees. Where we live in R.I., it does this every afternoon right before suppertime. Like the birds chirping with the morning sun, you can practically set your watch to it. Grams calls it the "four o'clock hurricane."

"Chill in the air, baby. Kids will want to go swimming. Why'd you have to start the party so late in the day?"

Poor Grams. I know she's tired from working two double shifts this week. They called her in this morning, too. She'd probably love it if she could just go home, lie on the couch, and watch the game.

"Here, sit in the sun," I tell her. "Adam's helping me. You don't have to do anything."

Adam got here about ten minutes ago to set up the volleyball net and the grill. He's wearing a red and black Hawaiian shirt and jeans. I hated asking him, since I know he went clamming all day, but there's so much to do and nobody else to help do it.

The thing is, Claire talked me into having this party, but then she and Nellie had to go to one of their relative's picnics at the last minute. A very lame excuse, if you ask me. She's promised to help when she gets here (*if* she gets here), but I need her to help me now!

Maybe it's best not to count on her for anything anymore.

My brother and I make a million trips back and forth to our house. Miles pushes the wheelbarrow with cans of soda and bags of chips and the decorations, while I carry the hamburger and hotdog rolls and condiments and paper goods.

There are three picnic tables at our beach, so I don't have to stress about that, but we need to use heavy buckets of sand and seashells to stop the tablecloths from blowing away in the wind.

Adam agreed to be in charge of the music, too, which is awesome, but he's having trouble with the extension cord, so he has to run back home to get another.

After he leaves, I take a break, sitting at one of the tables. The river is busy this afternoon, with kids and families enjoying the last weekend before we have to go back to school. Some kids are swimming out to the floating wooden dock, where Claire and I used to pretend we were bikini models back in the day. Not anymore.

Despite all her promises to hang out more often, she ditched me again the other night to go out with Adam, and it's not even like she's in love with him—not like I am with Trey. Here's what she told me when we were at the mall:

Adam's almost too nice, Sid. Some days I really like him. Other days I don't think I'm ready to like anybody yet.

Doesn't she get how lucky she is?

I've been tripping for days about my boyfriend, because I still, still, *still* haven't heard from him. I can't believe it was exactly one year ago today that we were getting ready to say good-bye. He took me out to the Clam Shack to celebrate our birthdays—my Sweet Sixteen. We sat on the edge of the deck at the restaurant, holding hands, trying not to dwell on the obvious. At that point we'd been going out for four months, which means I've been waiting for Trey three times longer than the total time we spent together.

(I guess if love were a math problem, the answer wouldn't seem very logical.)

Adam's come back now and is setting up the speakers. I've put Miles in charge of filling the water balloons and making sure people know where to put their supplies for the troops. This way he's got something to do till my cousins get here.

Oh, and my father called this morning and said his car broke down, and he and Tanya were stuck in North Carolina, so I don't have to worry about him expecting me to drop everything to see him tonight. This should make me feel happy, but it doesn't. Not really.

It's after five now, and I'm starting to stress that nobody is going to show when, sweet relief, a whole group of my friends pull up in their cars.

Sasha and Joe from chorus bring a box of Power Bars for the troops. And Laura and Brooke (from the Eye-Scream store) are here, too. Eric and Gillian, who have been going out since eighth grade, bring a few bags of chips and some salsa.

"We just got out of work," says Brooke, handing me a birthday present. They got me a gift certificate to the mall and a cute pair of silver hoop earrings.

"You guys didn't have to get me anything!"

"We know. We *wanted* to. Happy birthday. Sorry about Trey not coming home." They're so nice, and it's so good to see them—know what I'm saying?—it makes me feel really special.

Everybody heads to my house to change into their bathing suits (except the boys, who are already wearing theirs). When we come back, Joe and Eric begin throwing the girls into the river. The girls are kicking up their legs, and Brooke is screaming. Everyone is having a great time.

I've got on my favorite aqua and black bikini, so I run and jump in before they can throw me in—but then Miles comes along with his pail of balloons, and total chaos breaks out. The boys take turns bombarding me, so I duck under the water.

"One. Two . . . Six. Seven. Eight . . ." They're trying to hit me seventeen times.

"Okay, stop. I give up! I'm getting out."

Wrapping a towel around myself, I sit and watch all of my friends having fun. This party is turning out awesome, I think. That is, until I see Eric making out with Gillian all p.d.a.-ish, which makes me start obsessing about Trey. Before I start bawling my eyes out again, I decide to call his sister.

Trey told me that if the troops aren't out patrolling, they usually get a chance to call home on their birthdays. I have a feeling his family might have heard from him today. Besides, this morning my horoscope said, "Look for a message from far away."

With my friends being all crazy and wild, it's too noisy near the water. So I take my phone out to the street and punch in Trey's house number, which I happen to have on speed dial. His sister answers on the first ring.

"Latisha? It's Sid."

"Oh, hi."

She doesn't seem very excited to hear from me, but I keep talking anyway.

"Hey, listen. Your brother hasn't been in touch with me in, like, almost two weeks. It's not like him at all. I mean it's his birthday, right? Have ya'll heard from him today?"

"Oh." She pauses. "I'm sorry, Sid. I didn't want to be the one to tell you this—"

"Tell me *what*?" But I can tell by the tone of her voice, and the sick feeling which begins in the pit of my stomach and travels in crashing waves up my spine. Whatever it is, it isn't gonna be good.

ADAM

6:30 P.M. "Hey, Adam." Miles smiles when he sees me and offers his knuckles for a fist bump. His front tooth is missing, but his apple cheeks are all plumped up in a smile. In my opinion, Sid's brother is one cool little kid. He's got on these fake Oakley sunglasses and a green army shirt, which is hanging down to his knees. And he's got all these crazy dance moves for every song on my playlist—a regular party animal.

"Collecting any good stuff for the troops, Miles?"

"Oh, yeah. Suntan lotion. Energy bars. Coffee. Razors. Phone cards. Look at all this good stuff."

"Well, your big sister will be happy about that." I'm thinking Sid's going to need more than a few cardboard boxes to send off all of these supplies. At least thirty people are here already—and she was worried no one would come.

But I can't help but notice that one "certain someone" hasn't yet made her appearance. "Hey, you didn't happen to see Claire sneak by here, did you, Miles?"

"Nope."

I ask this because I'm running out of daylight. I'm also kind of pissed about the conversation Claire and I had this morning. Part of the continuing, my-dad-doesn't-like-you conversation. She called me around ten, all upset.

Supposedly her father had "issues" with me being at the party.

What do you mean issues, Claire?

It still bothers him. The whole keg thing. He might not even let us go. I was thinking. If I can get him to change his mind, could you just sort of disappear when he's dropping us off?

Silence. On my end.

Fish? Are you still there?

Yeah.

Well, anyway. See you later, hopefully, maybe, okay?

Yeah, okay.

But it's past six-thirty, and she's still not here. Sid said she was coming, but maybe she decided not to, or her dad wouldn't let her, which means—I don't know what it means.

Correction: One thing it means is that she finally told her dad about us. But seriously, who does he think he is? The judge of me, apparently. Is he perfect or something? Hasn't he ever made a mistake? Hasn't he ever screwed up?

Which reminds me—I left my own father sleeping in front of the TV this afternoon. Ever since Pop got back from his last fishing trip, he's been flat-out with a case of bronchitis. Three days of pouring-down rain in the middle of the ocean can get you that way. I borrowed his truck to bring a grill to the party. And left a note—next to the cough syrup—so he wouldn't think somebody stole his precious wheels.

The sun is blazing low in the sky. I decide to stop thinking about Claire and enjoy the moment. Looking around, I see everybody chillin' to my mellow mix of tunes, and I'm positive this has turned out to be a good party after all. So what if I've been stuck flipping burgers while Sid's grandmother dozes off in a chair? So what if I'm in charge of stoking the fire pit so there'll be nice hot embers when it gets dark?

I'm thinking it's worth it for Sid, because Sid always listens to me and never makes fun of my license plates (sorry, but that still irks me), and Sid isn't ever embarrassed that I'm one of her friends.

So yeah, I'm feeling real good and relaxed as I grab another Diet Coke from the cooler and a burger from the grill. I wander around, making sure people have enough to eat and say "hey" to more kids as they drop by.

Probably that's why I'm completely unprepared for what happens next.

Out on the river, someone is roaring around on a Jet Ski—and he's getting way too close to the dock.

What the hell?

We've seen water-skiers and boats up and down the river all afternoon, but this dude is being totally reckless. I mean, some of Sid's cousins, little kids, are swimming out there. They're screaming for him to get away. "Stop! Stop!"

"Adam? Who's that?" Miles has noticed him, too.

"I don't know, little dude." The sun is shining directly into my eyes, so it's hard to see. I might need a different view. "Be right back."

I'm about to run down there and tell that asshole to get lost when the kid on the Jet Ski makes a turn and heads for the sandy beach. There's a huge stream of water shooting up behind him, which is the last thing I see before I trip over a cooler and fall.

With my luck, it just figures, right?

But from this angle, I feel my jaw clench and my fist get tight, because now I know for sure who it is—before he even sets foot on the sand.

CLAIRE

6:36 P.M. After my father drops us off, we see Sid right away. She's on the street with a red beach towel wrapped around her waist and her Sidekick glued to her ear. She barely acknowledges my presence (or Nellie's), just waves us away with an angry "NOT NOW!" before we can even wish her a happy birthday or give her our gift or anything.

Is she mad because we're late to her party? I mean, obviously we couldn't help it—sometimes family stuff has to come first.

(Sometimes family stuff isn't so bad.)

Nellie skips ahead to say hi to Miles, who is near the collection boxes, while I say hello to Lonnie and Max and a few people I know from school. After a couple of minutes, Nellie pulls down her shorts (with her silvery bikini underneath) and heads down to the water for a swim.

I'm right behind her, taking off my navy blue hoodie because she obviously can't go swimming alone. But beyond her, looking at the water with his arms crossed, is Adam.

"Hey, you!" I say, running over to him.

But like Sid, he doesn't seem very happy to see me. "Oh,

236

hi," he says tensely. He takes a bite of a cheeseburger, wiping his mouth with the back of his hand.

"What's wrong? Aren't you glad that Nellie convinced my dad to let us come?" He just stares. At the water. At a Jet Ski. *Fantastic.*

A group of Sid's friends from work are gathered around Nick's black Jet Ski, the one he got last year, with its bright yellow stripe on the side. I'm upset, obviously, yet for some reason I'm not that surprised to see him here.

But I've never seen Fish this angry. "You didn't tell that tool about the party, did you?" he asks.

"Of course not. We ran into Meredith at the mall last week. She probably said something." Although, as I look around, I can see some kids eating burgers and others playing volleyball—but no Meredith.

"Just so you know, if he's staying, I'm not," says Adam, sulking.

"Don't be ridiculous. I'll go talk to him. Just let me handle it, okay?"

I run down to the beach, where Nellie is building a castle with some of Sid's younger cousins. Out on the river, I notice another Jet Ski. It's R.J. and he's got a tenth-grader named Audrey on the back. He drops her off at the shore, where she splashes over to some boys.

As soon as Nick sees me, he can't come over fast enough. He moves through the water with long wide strides. "Hey, baby," he says, as if we're not even broken up. As if I'm going to jump for joy that he's here.

And damn. There's that familiar flutter inside. Will it ever go away?

"Nick. How are you?" I'm trying my best to sound disinterested, but when he gives me that sexy grin, it's almost like old times. He asks what I've been up to, and I tell him about coaching at the gym, and how it's been helping me. He says he's been digging holes for a landscaper this summer. The conversation is going so well that I'm thinking maybe we can be friends—but then I hear some kids yelling and screaming in the distance, and one of them sounds like my sister.

Eric and some kid I don't know (with a huge tattoo on his shoulder) are playing chicken about halfway out to the diving platform. Gillian is straddled up on Eric's shoulders, and Nellie is splashing water up at them. "Wanna play too!"

Nick nods in her direction. "By the way, your sister looks great. She's pretty much back to normal now, huh?"

I suppose if you didn't know all the things that were still wrong with her, my sister could look pretty normal. Nick probably can't tell that she's laughing too loud or standing too close to tattoo-boy, who keeps nervously backing away from her.

"She's making progress," I reply. "I should probably go get her."

But I wait a minute to see how she's going to handle this.

I must be distracted watching her, because the next thing I know, Nick is beside me with his big heavy arm draped over my shoulder, pulling me close. He actually has the nerve to start kissing my neck.

"Could you not?" I say, trying to pry him off of me.

"Don't be like that, Claire," he says, letting go. On his breath is a hint of beer. "Won't be long now till I'm away at college. I'm leaving Monday. Maybe you could stay over sometime? Boston's not too far of a drive."

"Really? Well, first of all, I don't have my license anymore, remember? And second, I thought Meredith was doing that."

Nick turns red and squirms. "She likes to think so. But she's not you. No one will ever be you, Claire. I miss you. A lot." He almost seems sincere. "Don't you miss me? Even a little?"

Do I?

Actually, amazingly, the answer to that question is no. I don't miss his getting wasted, or the way he made me feel like I was constantly under his spell. We might have had something once, but it's totally over now. I'm just about to tell him that when I feel someone come up behind me.

"Everything okay here?" says Adam, pressing his body against mine.

I'm really nervous about the two of them facing each other again, but then Nick sticks out his hand, like they're long-lost friends.

"Fish-man? How's it hanging?"

Adam glares at him as if he's crazy.

"Come on. I'm so over it, dude. R.J. is, too. No hard feelings, okay?" Nick offers his hand again, like he's actually sorry.

For some reason Adam decides to shake it, but at the last second, Nick jerks his hand away.

"My bad." Nick slaps his thigh, laughing. "Can't believe you fell for that, dude."

"Whatever." Adam is furious now. He points a finger at Nick. "You need to bounce. This is a private party. Last time I checked, you weren't on the guest list."

Nick moves closer to me. "Well, I might go soon, bro. But,

I'm not finished talking to my woman here yet."

"Really?" Adam shifts an eyebrow. "I'm pretty sure she's not your woman, anymore." Then he looks at me. "Right?"

Okay, so this is when I should have probably said something to agree with Adam.

But I didn't want there to be a scene, not at Sid's birthday party, not after what happened the last time these two got into a fight.

So I keep quiet—but of course that turns out to be completely the wrong decision.

"Hah! She just dissed you, dude," says Nick, taunting.

"Right. Keep talking, dude. You'll say something intelligent eventually."

"What the—" Nick puffs up and pushes Adam's shoulder.

Adam pushes him back harder, and Nick stumbles down the steep bank. Then Adam pulls back a fist like he's going to go after him.

"Stop it! Both of you!" I'm standing in front of Adam, trying to block his way, when R.J. roars up onto the beach on the Jet Ski. He's got his hair cut in a fresh Mohawk, which I think looks ridiculous on his tiny bald head. But at least he distracts them.

He guns the throttle. "Let's go, Nick. This party is lame. You seen Audrey? I think she's got some beers in her cooler."

Nick doesn't want to back down yet, I can tell. But when Audrey comes out of the water, she's dripping wet with this very nice body, and did I mention she's wearing a see-through beige bikini?

"You freaks deserve each other," Nick mutters. "Hey,

Audrey!" he yells. "Wanna go party?"

"Yeah!" Audrey dries herself off with a towel. "Let me go get my stuff!"

Nick walks over and starts up the motor.

Near the picnic table, Audrey ties a batik-print skirt around her waist and picks up her canvas tote cooler. After she prances through the water, Nick grabs her hand, and he lifts her onto his Jet Ski. She wraps her arms around his chest.

We watch as both Jet Skis circle once around the dock and then take off down the river.

Now that Nick is gone, I'm thinking we can finally relax. But when I look at Adam, he still seems tense. He won't even meet my eye.

"Thanks for that just now," he says sarcastically.

He means about me being his girlfriend, I guess, which I totally need to explain. "Listen, I know. About that. I'm sor—"

"Don't, okay?" Adam glances at the grill near the tables. "Look, I've got some burgers to check on, and then I'm gonna roll."

"What? But I thought we were . . . I mean, I just got here!"

"Yeah, but I've got a curfew, remember?"

I can't believe this is happening. "Please stay, Adam. We need to talk."

But he's already got out his car keys. I didn't realize it was getting so late. And with the sun going down, I can almost feel the temperature dropping. Most of the other kids are coming out of the water now, including my sister.

"Hurry up, Claire!" she screams. She's hopping up and

down on one foot, with her arms to her chest. "Freezin' out. Where my clothes? Need towel!"

Oh, joy. Where did she leave her stuff? "Be right there!" I yell, hoping she heard me.

Adam pauses. "Funny. I thought you wanted to talk to me."

I touch his arm. "Listen. You know I've got to take care of her first. I'll be back in a minute. Wait here, okay?"

Then, just for spite, I guess, he pulls a cigarette out of his pocket and lights up—right in front of me! He blows a smoke ring into the space between us.

"Sorry, but it feels like you're playing me, Claire."

SID

6:36 P.M. "Stop playing around, Latisha. Tell me what happened to him!"

I'm still on the phone with Trey's sister, who's been stalling for the past half an hour, or at least that's how it feels, until finally she can't keep it from me any longer.

"Look. Nothing happened *to* him, Sid. It's just that, well, he's been seeing somebody else. In Iraq. Another girl. She's a nurse over there. I guess that's why my dumb brother hasn't called you. Sorry to be the one to tell you this. But you asked. And I guess you have a right to know."

I am so shocked . . . so completely stunned. . . .

She keeps going. "Sid? Are you there? He just got lonely. Don't blame him. It's an awful place. Take care of yourself, okay?" And then she hangs up.

For a few minutes I hold the phone in my hand, staring at it like, *What just happened here? How can this be?*

I know Trey hasn't been in touch with me lately, but I figured that was just because he was upset about not coming home. Now I can't help wondering, maybe he's really just staying there because of her.

The people here are almost more like my family now. Understand?

But I thought Trey's family was going to be *my* family! I thought what we had together was real. But now . . . I feel so alone now. Even more alone than when we first left my mom in the group home; more betrayed than when my dad first moved to Florida. I honestly don't know where I belong.

Actually, I'm sure I *don't* belong back at my party. Not feeling like this. Not where people are laughing and having fun. Why did I ever let Claire talk me into still having this stupid party?

I sit up against the telephone pole and begin bawling my eyes out for real. I don't know how long I stay like this, but it must be a while because it's almost dark, and I've almost stopped crying, when Claire suddenly appears in her faded blue shorts and hoodie, running toward me.

We've always had this psychic connection—she must have sensed that I needed my best friend! But before I can even get out the words, she's totally jogged past me in her flip flops and—*what the heck?*—it looks like she's not going to stop!

"Claire, wait!"

She yells back over her shoulder, "Nellie just got out of the water, Sid. She's freezing. Sorry we were late to your party. Happy birthday!"

"But Claire—" Doesn't she realize something terrible has just happened?

"I'll be right back! Pearl said you've got extra towels on the porch. My sister will be up here in a couple of minutes. Make sure she doesn't wander into the street, okay?" Her long red hair is swaying back and forth as she turns the corner for my house.

And before I can even get over that, Adam charges by on the other side of the street, arms pumping—heading straight for his dad's truck. He's in such a hurry, I don't think he even notices me.

"Adam, wait!"

But unlike Claire, when he sees me, he slows down. And unlike Claire, he is definitely stopping to talk. I'm just about to tell him about Trey when Adam blurts out that he just had a fight with Claire. "That tool had his arm around her, Sid!"

"What? Who?"

"Nick."

"Nick is *here*?"

He goes on, telling me how Nick *was* here, but he's not anymore. And how Adam is convinced that Claire is totally messing with his head. I feel so bad for him.

"Don't worry, Adam. She knows how lucky she is to have you. You're a good boyfriend. Really."

"She told you that?"

"Well, no . . . not exactly."

"Right." He frowns. "Well, what if I'm not ever good *enough*, Sid? She told me that I might want to disappear when her dad dropped her off today. And when Nick said she was *his woman*, she didn't even try to set him straight. What is her problem, anyway?"

He lights a cigarette, coughs, and then stands there like I should be able to offer some kind of an explanation.

I can't. I think it's ridiculous that Claire would go and hurt him like this. I don't care how much she's been through this summer; instead of making her stronger, like Grams says, I think this whole experience has made her selfish and weak. Or maybe she was always that way—and I never noticed.

"Well, I wasn't going to say anything, Adam, but the other day? She told me she might not be ready to like anyone yet."

"What?" He looks devastated.

"I'm sorry. But you deserve better."

I'm also thinking that maybe I deserve better, too.

Adam must pick up on the catch in my voice, because he looks into my eyes and really stares. "Sid, what's wrong? Have you been crying?"

So I tell him my whole sad, tragic story.

"Basically I've been dumped. And he didn't even have the balls to tell me himself. And the worst thing is, I think I still love him. What am I going to do?"

Adam seems upset and a little embarrassed. "Why didn't you say any of this before, Sid? You let me go on and on about my stupid fight with Claire."

"Oh, you didn't know. How could you? Actually, Claire came by here a minute ago. And kept right on walking. I mean, she saw how upset I was, but she didn't even bother to ask what was wrong!"

"Whoa." He raises his eyebrows skeptically. "I seriously don't get her at all."

My stomach feels sort of queasy. I don't feel like talking about Claire anymore.

"Adam, do you think you could just hold me? I could really use a friend right now. And you're about the only true friend I've got. Please?"

"Aww, poor Sid. Come here." Adam hugs me, a long full-body hug that feels so good and comforting—it almost makes some of my hurt disappear.

Until we hear the gravel shuffle behind us. We quickly pull apart and turn around.

Claire looks first at me and then at Adam. Her eyes glint in the dark, like fishhooks. "What the hell's going on?"

CLAIRE

7:16 P.M. "It's not what you think," Sid replies when I discover the two of them together. As in, *together* together. Adam guiltily looks away.

"Okay, then, what was it, Sid?"

"A hug, Claire. A simple hug. You know, that thing that friends give each other when they're upset?" Her pale green eyes stare back at me, looking justified somehow.

I want to believe her, but I've gotten pretty good at reading people these days—and it didn't look like a simple hug. In fact, right now, Adam's silence says more than if he tried to deny it.

Unbelievable. I'm getting this sinking, jealous, desperate . . . and really *pissed off* feeling as I hug the towels to my chest.

"I can't believe you guys would do this to me!"

"Do what?" Sid is instantly defensive. "Be there for you? Because that's all we have *ever* done. It's not always all about you, Claire! I'm so sick of your selfish drama! Ever since the accident, you've been like this. Maybe even before. Despite what you think, the world doesn't always revolve around *you*!"

"Around *me*?" It feels like I've been punched in the chest.

I can't believe Sid would say something so hurtful, so mean. Out of anyone, she should know what I've been through this summer. How the hell does she expect me to act? To feel?

"Are you serious, Sid? Like I don't know that? Is that what you guys really think?"

Neither one of them answers, which is ten times worse than if they tried to take it back. Apparently that's *exactly* what they think.

How ridiculous was I, thinking I could have a normal life again? And that the two of them would try to help me? Obviously, I'm better off hiding in my room—or at the gym. If my so-called friends can do this to me, I'd rather be alone for the rest of my life.

This is crazy. I need to get my sister, find our stuff, and go home.

It's getting dark out; a car goes by with the headlights on. Adam tosses his keys in his hand. Then Sid rewraps her towel around her waist, and I glance over near the parked cars for my sister, but she doesn't seem to be there like I expected.

I wish I never had to speak a word to either of them ever again, but I sort of have to if I want to go home.

"So where's Nellie, Sid?"

"How should I know?" she snaps.

"I asked you to keep an eye on her, remember?"

"What? No, you didn't! You told me not to let her wander into the street. She hasn't been by here." Sid bends her leg and rubs some gravel off the bottom of her foot. Adam swats a mosquito on his arm.

"So let me get this straight. Neither of you knows where she is?"

They look at me blankly.

"Fantastic," I say. "Well, thanks for nothing."

Needles of anxiety prick my whole body, but I try to stay calm. Nellie is probably fine. A group of kids are standing around the glowing fire pit. From here, it's hard to tell who's there, but if my sister wanted to get warm . . .

"Later," I say.

Sand is flying up against my shins as I run down the beach. Turning once, I notice that Sid and Adam are running right behind me, not that I care.

Suddenly, I feel a tug when Sid grabs my jacket sleeve. "Claire, wait."

I pause. "Why? So you can stab me in the back again?"

"No. Listen. I didn't know you needed me to watch Nellie. And I just got the most horrible news. Trey's been seeing someone else!"

"Where? In Iraq?" I can barely process this information.

"Yeah, I thought he was busy or I didn't know what to think when I hadn't heard from him. Latisha told me on the phone when I called their house tonight. And honestly Adam was just trying to calm me down."

She looks so upset that I know she's telling the truth. Fish is standing off to the side, watching us. He takes a pack of cigarettes out of his pocket, but when he sees me glare at him, he puts them away.

"I'm so stupid," Sid says, sniffling. "And the worst part is—"

"Sid, wait a minute, okay?" I know she wants me to hear the whole story, but I'm sort of in the middle of panicking at the moment. "Look, I don't mean to be rude, but I really need to look for—"

She dabs at her nose with the edge of her towel. "Sorry. We'll help you, okay?"

It doesn't make sense. My sister's not at the fire pit, like I was completely sure she would be. Where could she have gone?

Fish looks worried. "What do you want us to do?"

"*Find her,*" I say, trying not to sound too mean.

"You don't think she went for another swim?" Sid asks ominously.

We all stare at the river, scanning the water, which is dark and deep and over your head past the floating swimming dock. "No. I don't think so," I say.

I'm pretty sure Nellie wouldn't have gone back in, not after she said she was so cold. But then, where the hell did she go?

Adam wonders if she could have gotten lost somehow in the neighborhood. Or wandered over to Sid's house? He offers to drive around and look for her, but I think we should make sure she's not here first.

"I'm going to get more people to help us," he says, determined.

I start to scream. "Nellie? Where are you??? Nellie!!!" Then we're all running down the beach, shouting and screaming her name. I'm going crazy trying to see in the dark.

There is an empty wooded lot along the banks of the river. When we were in middle school, some of us liked to play manhunt in there. I call over to Gillian and Eric, but they don't think anyone is playing manhunt right now.

I yell at the woods anyway, because what if she's hiding for fun?

"Nellie? This isn't funny! If you can hear me, you better

come out. RIGHT NOW!" But no one calls back. Nothing happens.

I'm just about to give up and call my parents when Miles trots over to us out of the darkness. It looks like he's been eating a hot dog, because flecks of yellow mustard stain his cheek.

"Hey, you guys looking for Nellie?" he asks innocently.

"Oh my god! Yes, Miles. Where is she? Have you seen her?"

"Yeah, maybe. I think so." Miles nods with eyes that are brown and round and scared. "Didn't she leave with that kid on the Jet Ski?"

NELLIE'S BRAIN

7:17 P.M. *C'est incroyable.* One minute we were standing there peacefully looking at the sunset . . . and the next?

We are roaring and bumping through the cold, black river water in the foamy wake of the other Jet Ski, which is darting back and forth, zig-zagging in front of us.

Nellie is thinking, *This is fun!*

The Boy reminds her, "Hold on to me, now. Tight."

It may be fun, *mes amis*, but you would probably agree, it is definitely *not* the greatest idea.

With the wind in her face and the riverbanks on either side, our girl turns her head, reassured because she can still see the flicker of the fire pit at the party. Sid's party. She does not want to go too far. The Boy promised they would not go too far. But just like that, they veer around a bend, and the light is gone.

The Jet Skis tear along a wide stretch of river now, past big houses lit from the inside and long, splintery docks— then *whoosh*, just like that, the houses and the docks are gone, too.

Under the bridge and around the pylons the Boys race

each other, as if on motorcycles, to the open, choppy water and the vast expanse of the bay. We have left the river behind us. Tonight the Narragansett seems *ènorme,* with swells and whitecaps, almost like the ocean. In the distance, Nellie can see a lighthouse, and beyond that a large gray tanker which is possibly transporting fuel from Quonset Point.

The last sliver of sun disappears from the horizon. As it does, Nellie can see other lights far, far off, twinkling on the opposite shore. She does not want to be scared by what is happening, but she is. *Elle avait l'air effrayé.* Very scared.

How did she get into this mess?

Our girl had been standing on the beach earlier, feeling warm (or warm enough) wrapped in the towel Miles had given her, watching the sunset and the pink clouds—which were the color of that fluffy stuff you might purchase at a fair—when one of the Jet Skis roared back onto the shore.

Not Nick's Jet Ski, the other Boy's. Nellie had noticed him frolicking about on it earlier. It had looked like such fun! And she thought she knew him, too, with that Mohawk of hair down the center of his head. What was his name again?

Something with letters like PJ or TJ? He was somewhat good-looking, in a long-legged, small-headed way. Maybe he could be her boyfriend someday?

She watched as he hopped off the big machine. "Audrey forgot her jacket," he said to her, shrugging. "Her phone's in the pocket. Have you seen it? It's blue."

"Maybe over there?" she replied, wanting to help.

There was a pile of clothing near one of the picnic tables. He went over and found what he was looking for quickly.

Then he waded through the water and got back onto his Jet Ski. *About to take off without her.*

Nellie knew she would not get another chance.

"Hey, could I have ride?"

(*Mes amis*, there was not a thing I could do to stop her.)

The Boy held onto her waist as he helped her get on the big machine. "I don't care what anybody says, Nellie. You still look mad-sexy to me."

Night falls hard and quick in Rhode Island at the end of the summer. Nellie cannot see much of anything now except for dark water around her. Her face is burrowed deep into R.J.'s shoulder—*that* is his name—and her arms are around his broad chest, trying to stay warm. Although the Boy's body is warm, and the Jet Ski is thrumming, our girl's bathing suit is damp, and her teeth are chattering. (And we know how Nellie hates to be cold.)

Status report: Nellie cannot remember if she told Claire that she was going for a ride. She thinks: *probably not.* This means that Claire is going to be mad, so mad at her. How is she going to explain?

"GO BACK NOW, 'K?" Nellie yells, but her words fly away in the wind.

"WHAT? I CAN'T HEAR YOU! THE MOTOR'S TOO NOISY!"

The waves of the bay splash up around them. Precarious waves, like speed bumps in the water. With every *thump, thump, thump*, I am afraid Nellie might lose her balance and fall in.

At last, Nick's Jet Ski turns into a small cove, a hidden beach, surrounded by pine trees. R.J. is right behind him. There are jagged rocks in this cove, so they cannot coast onto the sand. Nick hops off first, waist-deep in water, and helps Audrey with the pretty black hair. Lifting the hatch on the Jet Ski, he pulls out a cooler. They wade through the shallow water, pulling the machine to shore.

R.J. gets into the water, too. It is quiet now, with the motors turned off. Nellie thinks maybe she can tell him how she is feeling. He has to understand. "I'm cole. Claire's gonna worry. Wanna go back now, 'K?"

"Not yet," R.J. tells her. "We've got a surprise for you girls. You'll see. Come with me."

At first she refuses to get off; it is dark water, scary. Tiny black flies squeal at her head. But the Boy will not go anywhere without her.

"What now?" He slaps his long neck, where a mosquito has landed. "You're gonna make me wait here all night?"

"Slimy," she says, pointing at the green seaweed. *Répugnant.*

"Fine," he says. "You weigh next to nothing. I'll carry you." His hand grips at her thigh too tightly, but he carries her over his shoulder, pulling the Jet Ski behind him. When he puts her down on the sand, small stones poke at the soles of her feet.

The Boys use their cell phones to light the way. R.J. is pushing Nellie through the dark woods, which are thick with vines and scratchy branches, until they reach a small clearing.

"Nick loves to bring the ladies here," R.J. explains. "It's private as hell."

Under a plastic tarp, there is dry wood—some sticks and branches. Nick gathers it together into a pile and lights a match. "We'll have a fire soon." He takes a striped blanket from under there, too, and spreads it on the ground.

Leaning against a tree trunk, he pulls Audrey down close to nestle at his side. "Warm me up, *woman.*"

Audrey giggles. "Okay." She adjusts her skirt to cover her bare legs. Nellie wishes that she had some warm clothes.

Nick opens the cooler and takes out a six-pack. He throws a can to R.J. "You like parties, right, Nellie?"

She shrugs. "Maybe."

R.J. laughs as he snaps open the can. "Well, you were doing some sexy cartwheels at our last party. *Remember?*"

All of sudden Nellie *does* remember.

Did you ever do a Jell-O shot? I did, they're yummy.

Pass him, Claire. Pass him.

I want to flash him. Come on, Claire, please?

Nellie closes her eyes to stop the memories from coming, not sure she wants to remember anything else.

After a while, Nick and Audrey start kissing, noisily, passionately. It is not long before they are lying on top of each other with their legs intertwined. Audrey's black hair is getting messy from Nick's pawing.

Nick begins to moan. "Yeah, that's it, yeah."

Kind of disgusting, Nellie thinks, how all over each other they are. Audrey must be thinking the same thing. "Not here, Nick," she says. "Please?"

"Okay." Nick stands up and drains his can, tossing it into the bushes. "I know somewhere even better."

Nellie hopes that means they will be leaving this place. (Frankly, *mes amis*, I am hoping that very same thing.)

Nick grins. "It's not too far. We can walk."

Audrey reaches down to fold the blanket. "Don't do anything I wouldn't do, Nellie," she says, laughing. Putting his arm around her, Nick winks at R.J. before they disappear into the woods. "Later, people. Have fun."

Ten minutes have passed, and Nellie is sitting on one side of the smoky fire, and the Boy is on the other. There is the sound of crickets humming and branches crackling, but not much else. It is so quiet that Nellie can hear, in the distance, the gentle lapping of waves.

"These bugs are killing me," says R.J., scratching his arm. "Hey, for a girl, you don't talk much."

"Sorry," she replies. "I used to."

"That's okay," he says. "Most girls flap their gums too much anyway."

Reaching for another piece of wood, R.J. stares at her across the dying fire. "Aren't you getting cold over there? All by yourself?"

Nellie notices that, for such a tall Boy, he has a very small head. He is somewhat ugly, too. And he does not seem very smart, either. Why did she ever think he might be a nice boyfriend someday?

His big hand pats the sandy soil next to him. "Come sit over here by me, little Nells. I'll warm you up."

"No, thanks." She shivers. "Not that cole. We can go now, 'K?"

He makes a face. "If you moved around a little, you wouldn't be cold at all. Hey, I have an idea. You still do gymnastics, right? Why don't you try a split for me, sexy?"

I have a very bad feeling about this.

Yet, Nellie is thinking that perhaps he is right; gymnastics always *does* warm her up. And she wonders, what harm would it be if she did a few splits—or a cartwheel or two? She stands up and puts her hands on her waist.

R.J. leers at her over the embers. The pupils of his eyes are as black as the sky. "Come on. Yeah, that's nice, Nellie. Go on. Spread those legs."

ADAM

7:37 P.M. "Which way, Miles?" asks Claire. "Which *way?* Think!"

Sid frowns. "He's already said he's not sure, Claire."

There's less than an hour till my curfew; twenty-three minutes to be exact. Instead of the three of us standing around waiting for a little kid to direct us, we could actually be *doing* something to find her. So I pull out the keys to my father's truck and head toward the street.

"Adam!" Sid yells. "You're not leaving us *now?*"

Claire looks upset. "It's fine, Sid. Just let him go."

"Hold on, both of you," I explain. "How else do you expect me to get my boat?"

They look at each other, then back at me. "Hurry up!"

It's only a two-minute drive from Sid's house to my house. If I hadn't had to bring the grill (and all that other stuff) to the party, I could've walked. But there's no time. I burn rubber as I pull away from the curb.

Three blocks. Two stop signs. One long driveway. Now, I'm running through the field to our dock, pulling up the small anchor, untying the mooring line, waiting for the engine to warm up before I push the throttle. As I wait, I mutter my usual mantra: *Don't stall, man, don't you dare stall.*

There's no time to clean out the mess: rakes, buckets, empty water bottles. I go back into the cabin and get behind the wheel.

It takes longer by boat to get back to Sid's beach. That's because I have to steer out to deeper water before letting her rip. A crater-filled moon begins to rise over the treetops, and I can't help remembering another full moon, on another night just like this one. It's not a memory that comforts me, but at least the moonlight will help us see.

As my boat slowly chugs along, I feel like I'm going to explode. I'm so pissed off at those idiots for taking Nellie. Who knows where they went or what they're doing to her? I know these waters like the back of my hand, but this river is three goddamn miles too long. And the bay is . . . endless.

How the hell will we ever find her?

When I get around the last section of thick marsh grass, Claire and Sid are waiting for me on the small beach, along with half the people from the party. I stand there with the motor idling, but they aren't coming out. "What's the problem?"

"Claire called her dad," Sid says, frowning. "Grams called the police. They should be here any minute. The harbormaster, too."

"Okay." I'm confused. "So are we *not* going now?"

"No, we have to!" Claire has this real panicky sound to her voice. "Unless you don't think you should."

"What about your curfew?" Sid says. "The police?"

It's nice of them to worry, but I shake my head. "Are you serious? We have *way* more important things to think about right now."

SID

8:15 P.M. I've never been out on Adam's boat before, or *any* boat, actually. In any other situation, I can see where it'd be kind of fun. It's amazing how at ease Adam is on the water. He steers us all expertlike past buoys that clang like bells.

It's such a clear night. Overhead, the stars are so vast in the dark summer sky that I feel like just a tiny dot in the universe, which is making me forget (or almost forget) about my broken heart.

Do they see the same stars in Tikrit? Trey told me once that they have different constellations. It's hard to believe he's not my boyfriend anymore—I've got to stop thinking about Trey!

My cell phone vibrates with a text.

I text back: no grams. didn't find her yet

We've been up and down the river twice, with no sign of those Jet Skis, when Claire mentions that Nick brought her over to this cove one time, on the other side of the point. She thinks maybe we should try there.

"Let's go," Adam agrees. He takes us under the bridge with the tiny green and red lights flashing. It's the channel into the bay. When we get into open water, Adam lets it fly. His boat goes *thud, thud, thud*, as it bangs over every swell. The waves here are bigger and choppier than in the river. And in the dark, the bay looks huge . . . like an ocean, which makes me think that Nellie could be anywhere.

Adam is up front in the cabin. Claire and I are sitting on the bench seat at the stern. My friend looks so lost with her hair blowing all wild, and with that puffy orange life jacket around her neck. I know she's hoping they took Nellie to that cove (we all are), but what are the odds of that being true?

Even if I'm worried, I've got to stay positive; that's what friends do. "The harbormaster will be out looking, too, Claire. Don't worry. Somebody's bound to find her."

She pats at the dry clothes we've brought for Nellie. Tears form in the corners of her eyes. "You don't understand, Sid. My father didn't want us to come tonight. We *have* to find her."

As Adam steers around the jutting coastline, he suddenly slows down. He sees something; he's pointing. I can't believe it, two Jet Skis!

"That's them!" Claire cries.

One of the Jet Skis has a yellow stripe, so it's definitely them.

Adam cuts the motor, and we begin drifting toward land. As he unties the anchor, he tells me to look around for a flashlight. But while I'm doing that, I hear a splash. Claire has dived off the boat, and she's swimming toward shore.

"Claire, don't," Adam shouts. "Wait for us!"

"No! You're taking too long. I'll yell when I find her!"

Adam throws the small anchor overboard. Then he

rummages in a storage bin and hands me a flashlight. After that, he picks up a big wooden clam rake and climbs down the ladder into the water. I'm not crazy about getting cold and wet again, but I guess I don't have much of a choice.

The first slimy step is the worst. The water is up to my thighs, cold and filled with icky seaweed. Who knows what else is down there that we can't see. Jellyfish? Crabs? (Not sharks. The water's too cold for sharks, I think.)

As we make our way around the rocks to the beach, Adam is moving so fast, I can barely keep up. He's also holding the rake high above his head, like you might carry a spear. It looks heavy and awkward. The tongs seem real sharp.

"Why did you bring that thing, anyway?" I ask.

"Don't worry about it, Sid," he replies with an edge to his voice. "It's just in case."

CLAIRE

8:45 P.M. "Claire?"

"Nellie? Is that you?!"

"Over here!"

My heart leaps. She's alive. Thank God, she's alive!

I realize, with a chill, that I must have been picturing my sister *not* alive. Like maybe she had fallen into the water and drowned, or they had left her somewhere alone—or something worse—I don't know. But we found her! And she's okay!

(At least she sounds okay.)

My hair is dripping wet and thorny vines cut at my legs as I run toward the sound of her voice. But when I find them together, in that small clearing, the first thing I notice is R.J. hopping around on one foot—in his underwear!

"What the *hell* are you doing?" I ask, although apparently he's been doing something very bad.

"It's not what you think," he replies, quickly pulling up his cargo shorts. "Nothing happened."

Funny, that's the second time someone has said that to me tonight. I'm pretty sure that Sid and Adam told me the truth—it's R.J. I don't believe.

But thank goodness, there's Nellie. She runs over and slams into me with a giant hug. "You found me! Sorry. Told him wanted to go."

I'm so happy and relieved to see her, but I'm beyond furious at R.J. and what he might have done. "You pig! What did you do to her?"

"Nothing, I swear! I wanted to, but . . . but . . . your sister's crazy. She just bit my hand!" He shakes his wrist and puts his hand to his mouth, then inspects it to see if it's bleeding.

I look over at my sister. "Is that true, Nellie? Are you all right? Did he touch you? Did you really bite his hand?"

"Had to," she says, shrugging. Her legs are covered with bloody bug bites and scratches. "Can take care of self, 'K?"

"Okay. But we're here. You're safe now."

I didn't notice at first, but Nick is standing a few feet away, and Audrey is with him. They have a blanket draped over their shoulders. Nick seems like maybe he's just now realizing the seriousness of the situation.

He glances quickly at my sister and then back at me. "She's really different now, huh?"

What an idiot. I hate him so much.

"Of course she's different, Nick. What do you expect? She had a brain injury! How could you just take off with her like that? Without telling anyone? And leave her alone with R.J.? We were all freaking out! Didn't you think anyone would wonder where she was?"

Behind us there's a sound of twigs snapping, and Adam and Sid rush into the clearing. Sid's got this bright flashlight, which she shines directly on R.J. He turns away from the glare.

"Adam!" cries Nellie. "Knew you would come." She runs over to him and throws her arms around his neck. In one hand he's carrying this big, heavy rake, which makes it kind of awkward for him to hug her back.

Adam glares at R.J. and Nick. "What's going on, Claire?"

Sid looks at me. "Is Nellie okay?"

"I think so." I hesitate. "But R.J.'s pants were down when I found them."

"What?!" Adam totally flips out. "I'm going to kill you, you crazy sick bastard!"

"No, don't!" I yell. "Maybe it's not what we think."

But it's too late. Adam starts swinging the rake. Audrey runs behind a bush, and Nellie comes back over to me. Nick and R.J. jump out of the way and laugh, somewhat nervously, like they don't believe he will actually hit them. But I do.

"He's nuts," says R.J., darting to the side where Audrey is cowering. "Come on." He grabs Audrey's hand and disappears with her into the woods.

Nick holds up his arms, like he's surrendering, when Adam blocks his way. "Stop! I didn't do anything, Fish, man. Stop playing around."

But Adam lunges at him again. "Like all those times you stopped, Nick?" He swings once more, closer to Nick's head this time. I'm really worried. It's like Adam wants to take revenge, not only for Nellie, but for everything bad that's ever happened to him—in his whole entire life.

Sid looks at me, terrified. "Claire, you've got to do something!"

She's right. I'm scared, but I take a breath and run behind Adam, ducking my head so I don't get hit. Then I grab onto his shirt, his right arm, and hold on.

"Adam, don't do this. It's not worth it!"

He tries to shake me off. "Get out of the way, Claire. He asked for it."

"No, he didn't. This is serious! You could kill him! Listen to me. Do the right thing, okay?"

Maybe that's what finally gets to him. Because when Adam turns around and looks at me, it's like he's coming out of a trance. Slowly, he puts the pole end of the rake down in the sand—like a flag.

"Fine, Claire. I give up. You win."

Nick reaches down and quickly grabs his keys from a log and takes off. "Later, freaks." We can hear the snapping of twigs as he runs away, and then it's just very quiet.

CLAIRE

9:30 P.M. We're on Adam's boat now, moving fast. Sid is sitting up in the cabin next to Adam, because I really wanted some alone-time with my sister.

"Don't like dark," Nellie says. We've both changed into dry clothes, but she's still shivering.

The moon has risen to a big white ball in the sky. It glitters off the foam in our wake. Behind us: mile after mile of watery darkness. On a night like this, it feels like the water could swallow you alive—you and all of your secrets.

Nellie scratches the mosquito bites on her leg and huddles under her towel. "Bad things happen at parties."

"I know, sweetie. Sorry I left you alone on the beach."

"'K." She nods. "Tried to show him my . . ." She looks down at her chest and starts to pull up her shirt.

I gently pull it down. "Don't do that, Nellie, okay?"

I was wondering if she'd be able to tell me what happened. "Did you flash him? Is that why R.J. thought he could—"

"Not R.J." She peers toward the front of the boat. "Adam."

"Adam?"

She lowers her voice to a whisper. "Shouldn't been drinking. Shouldn't have told you pass his car."

What? Is she talking about the accident? *Our* accident?

She pauses. "Not your fault about acc'dent, Claire."

A few months ago, when she could barely speak, I wondered if we'd ever be able to have this conversation . . . and now? I'm holding my breath.

I realize that it's time to tell her the truth about the accident. My truth. What I did to her. She deserves to know.

I wouldn't blame her if she hates me forever.

"Not your fault," my sister says again. "'Member? Told you to pass."

I exhale slowly. "Well, yes, it kind of *is* my fault, Nellie. I didn't have to pass Adam's car that night. Even if you told me to. I'm really sorry. I was the one driving—I wasn't being responsible. Maybe you're remembering some things, but you need to know this. I was sort of mad at you that night."

Nellie makes a face like a frown. "'Cause I was Dad's favorite, right? Center attention. Boys looking at me. You didn't like it."

I shake my head, amazed. "You knew about that?"

"Kinda obvious." She shrugs. "'K, well, I forgive you."

What? Just like that?

"For ever'thing. You didn't mean it." She pats my hand.

"I didn't?"

"No. Acc'dents happen, right?"

She's right. They do. And it *was* an accident. A terrible mistake. But how can my sister know all that I've taken from her, and incredibly, *unbelievably*, be willing to let it all go?

When I look at Nellie, she's staring into my eyes— and smiling.

I guess . . . maybe . . . it's because she loves me.

The accident didn't change that. Nothing will change that.

A part of me wants to say to her, *Think it over, you don't have to. I don't deserve it. If the situation were reversed, I'm not sure that I'd forgive you.*

But I don't. I can't.

Because, I realize, her forgiveness is a gift to *both* of us.

"You're right, Nellie. Accidents happen. And I'm so very, very sorry."

A few minutes later, Sid comes back to check on us. She says she texted her grandmother that we were all okay and on our way home.

"Grams said the police are on the beach waiting. They need to file a report. I should probably go back up and keep Adam company. He seems kinda upset."

"Yeah. Okay. Thanks, Sid."

As mad as I was at Nick and R.J., I'm grateful that Fish didn't hurt them—or kill them, or whatever he was trying to do. But he might be in trouble for breaking his curfew. Well, the cops will just have to understand.

I also realize that there are lots of worse things that could have happened tonight. Nellie is safe, but despite my sister's bravado back there, the way her brain works now makes her much more vulnerable—to all sorts of dangers.

"I'm really glad you're okay, Nellie. But you've got to be

more careful. You can't go off with random boys. You're sure R.J. didn't hurt you, right?"

"Right. But know what, Claire?" In the moonlight, her eyes are dancing. "Ever notice how R.J. has small head?"

I laugh. "Sid calls him a pin-head."

She smiles. "'Cause he's got a small you-know-what, too."

"What?" When I look at her sideways, she nods, giggling into her hand.

"*Seriously?*" I say, understanding exactly what she means.

Then we're both laughing, uncontrollable laughter, like we used to when we were little kids.

We're fast approaching the coastline, but I don't want this moment to ever end. And as I lean my head onto the softness of Nellie's shoulder, I have to wonder. How can it be possible for two sisters to go through the worst thing imaginable, and maybe, just maybe, come out of it okay?

A SEAGULL CAN OPEN A HARD CLAM BY CARRYING IT TO A HEIGHT OF FIFTY FEET AND DROPPING IT ON A ROCK OR OTHER HARD SURFACE. SOMETIMES IT HAS TO DO THIS SEVERAL TIMES BEFORE IT BREAKS.
—*Secrets of Shell Fishing*

ADAM

It's almost eleven by the time I pull up to our dock. I'm wired, but I get out, tie up, and decide to sit for a while. It's peaceful sitting here. Always has been. Even tonight.

Dozens of fireflies blink low to the ground. I remember reading once that fireflies blink with a specific light pattern in order to attract a mate. But that's not the only reason they glow—for their enemies, their light supposedly tastes really bad.

I've got an enemy. He's leaving on Monday for college.

With my luck, he'll probably flunk out and be back in two weeks.

Eventually, I notice the shadow of my dad standing at our front door. I yell to him that I'm down here. He walks across the lawn and through the field. He's wearing only a T-shirt and gym shorts—what he sleeps in.

He stops a few paces from where I'm sitting. And he doesn't look pleased. "You took the truck without asking. And then your boat was gone."

"I left a note, Pop. Didn't you see it?"

"Leaving a note's not the same thing as asking!" he snaps, and I guess he's right.

"Where were you so late, Adam? What, you got a couple months left? Why you wanna screw with it now?"

I let out a sigh. "Don't worry. The police said they won't even report me."

"*Police?*" He scratches his head like he knows he's missing most of the details, but where do I even begin?

"You might want to take a seat, Pop."

Fumbling for his pack, he lights up a smoke, shielding the flame with his big hands. A long, rattling cough resonates from deep within his lungs. Is that how I'll sound someday, if I don't quit?

As he listens, I tell him all about Sid's party and searching for Nellie, and how out of my mind I was that we wouldn't find her.

"You shoulda woke me up! I would've helped look!"

I shrug. "But we did find her, right? And when we got off the boat, Mr. Perry actually shook my hand. He even thanked me for taking care of his daughters."

"That's great, Adam."

Yeah, I'm real happy that Claire's father did that, too. And he was hugging both girls and telling them he loved them over and over. It was a nice family scene, which should've made me feel awesome. But remembering how close I came to erasing Nick's sneer from the face of the earth is suddenly freaking me out.

I decide to tell my father that part, too. "I wanted to bash his head in so badly, Pop. I could actually picture the blood. I can't believe how close I came. I mean, if Claire didn't stop me—I might have messed him up permanently."

Pop takes one last drag and flicks it in the water. "But you didn't, right? That's what counts. Some things aren't worth fighting for. You'd have to live with that for the rest of your life. Better to let the police handle it."

"I guess. But he'll probably get off. Nick always does. He didn't do anything 'enforceable.' Not really. So he took some girl out for a ride on a Jet Ski. It pisses me off. He always knows how to skate wicked-close to the edge—without ever having to pay the price."

My father mulls this over for a minute before he answers.

"I bet the universe will get him, eventually. You'll see. He'll lose something important. That's the only way some people can change. And take it from me, once that happens? The worst punishments are the ones we give ourselves."

His gaze is out past me now, toward the river. Maybe he's remembering a different summer's night? A night that changed *everything* for our family?

It's never too late to do the right thing.

"Pop? Do you think you'll ever get over what happened to Molly? I mean, we never talk about it. But I want you to know, I don't blame you. Not like Mom does, obviously. That's the real reason she left us, right?"

He takes the lighter out of his pocket again and begins flicking it, on and off.

"Dad?"

"You ever seen that movie *Jaws?* A shark holds this town hostage, out on the Vineyard. Keeps attacking people when they least expect it."

Where is he going with this? I hug my knees to my chest. "I think I saw a part of it one time. At Cookie's."

"Well, shame is like that," he says. "Like a shark. It can sneak up from behind you. Tear off a limb. Eat up all the space in your head. And what's worse? It can make you do even more things you're ashamed of—trying to appease it."

No wonder it's so hard to talk to him. He's always talking in riddles, dancing around the important stuff.

"Can't we just talk about what happened, Dad? Normally? Just this once?"

"Okay." He pauses. "I never told you this. But after your sister died, do you remember your mom and me fighting all the time?"

Who wouldn't remember that?

"I guess."

"Well, it was because your mom caught me doing something."

My head jerks up. "What are you talking about? Doing *what*?"

He hesitates. "I was so torn up. So desperate. I guess I found another woman to lose myself in. To help me forget. Okay, maybe it was more than just one."

I can't believe what he's saying. "What the hell, Dad?"

"I know. Crazy, right? What? You never liked two girls at the same time?"

He slaps my back, joking, but it's a little too hard. I almost lose my balance and fall right off the dock.

"Sorry, Adam. You okay? I know, dumb joke. Not the same thing, either. But learn from your old man's mistakes. Don't go cheating on any of your girlfriends, okay?"

"Okay, Pop," I say. "I'll keep that in mind."

We're both quiet again. Then he adds, "For the record,

your mother never blamed me for Molly. She blamed me for making her go through it alone. I'm not proud of that fact. Some mistakes are unforgivable. Maybe I didn't try hard enough to make it right. I'm not happy your mom left us, moving so far away—you didn't deserve that. But she was right to leave me."

A cargo ship's horn blasts; three long, low tones. We can see it, heading out of the harbor. I understand now why my father didn't want to tell me about the other women. It all makes sense. And even if it makes me sad for my parents—for all of us—I'm glad I finally know the truth.

Dad inches closer, patting my back. "So, when's that girlfriend of yours coming over for dinner? Maybe I can whip up some pasta and clam sauce?"

I laugh to myself. Like weather in New England—his mood never stays the same for very long.

I'd like to invite Claire over, but I'm not sure she'll agree to come. She was real upset when she found Sid and me together. Awkward. I wasn't too happy seeing her with Nick, either. We put it aside when we looked for her sister, but I have a feeling it's going to come up again. That, and my smoking, and her thinking I'm not good enough and . . .

"We're having a few issues at the moment," I reply. "I'll get back to you on that, okay?"

The boat thuds softly against the dock. My father looks at me curiously. "But she's nice to you? Makes you feel special?"

"Yeah, most of the time. But once in a while, I think she might be a little embarrassed of me."

"*Embarrassed?* What's she got to be embarrassed about?

You're a great kid. You shouldn't put up with that!"

"I know. We've got to talk. I want to work it out. I like her a lot."

He coughs again loudly, another long, wracking cough, which convinces me I've got to set a quit date and stick to it this time. It also gets me worried. Who's going to take care of him when I leave for college next year? I picture my dad rattling around in our house lonely or sick . . . or depressed.

"Pop? Didn't the doctor tell you to quit smoking? You're always coughing. That can't be good. How're you going to handle things next year, when I go away to college? I mean, who's going to help out if you get sick—or whatever?"

"Hmmm." He scratches his chin, hesitating. "Well, see. I never told you this before neither. But there's this lady I've been seeing. . . . She's from Fall River."

Just when I think this night can't get much crazier. "Were you planning to at least invite me to the wedding?"

He laughs nervously. "Didn't want to break the news till it was more *serious*. But since you're asking, her name's Mary. She don't like my smoking, either. She wants me to try the patch. Anyway, maybe I should bring her over sometime to meet you? What do you think? An old guy like me with a girlfriend—not too weird?"

I shake my head and put my arm around his shoulder. "No weirder than usual, Pop."

We watch as the lights from across the river bounce off the fast-moving current. If this river were music, I imagine it would sound like jazz. Or rhythm and blues. I'm thinking maybe a sax, a bass guitar, and drums with a smooth staccato beat.

It's amazing how this river never stops moving. It just never stops.

My father groans, stands up, and stretches his arms overhead. It's a beautiful night. The stars are so bright in the sky. "It's late. What do you say? You comin' in, buddy?"

Buddy? He hasn't called me that in years.

And when my father reaches down and offers me his hand—I decide to take it.

MRS. APPLETON'S CREATIVE WRITING
WRITE A PARAGRAPH ABOUT ONE OF
THE FOLLOWING PHRASES:
IN WAR, NO ONE REALLY WINS.
YOU SHOULD TRY TO LOVE YOUR ENEMIES.
REVENGE IS SWEET.
SUFFERING BUILDS A PERSON'S CHARACTER.

SID

"Hey, what's up . . ." says Claire as she pokes her head into my bedroom, ". . . with your room?" It's Sunday afternoon, the day after my party, and her mother has just dropped her off.

My room is actually kind of a dang mess at the moment, with my desk torn apart and piles of clothes on my bed and the floor. "I'm cleaning out old school stuff from last year. Look what I found from Mrs. Appleton's class."

I hand her the sheet of paper. After she reads it, I say, "She was nice. I'm gonna miss having her this year."

"Me, too," Claire agrees. She sits perched at the edge of my bed, with her bag over her shoulder. With that red polka-dot top and those black capri pants, she looks like a ladybug that might fly off any minute.

My grandmother insisted that I clean my room before I can go anywhere. She's even going to inspect it when she gets home to make sure.

School starts in three days, Sidonia. Get a fresh start!

I thought Claire and I should start our senior year with a fresh start, too. I was feeling guilty about what I said to her last night, so I'm glad she agreed to come over and talk. Why have something hanging over us again?

Before I can stop her, Claire picks up the small framed picture I have on my nightstand. The one I haven't packed away in my memory box yet.

"Oh," she says. "Have you heard anything more from—?"

"Not now, okay?"

It's not that I don't want to talk about Trey. When I got up this morning, our break-up hit me all over again. But Claire and I have some unfinished business to get out of the way first.

"Well, your new comforter is nice," she says, running her hand over one of the big yellow sunflowers. Both of us always did like sunflowers.

"Grams is hoping that all this decorating and reorganizing will inspire me to start on those college applications."

"Yeah. I hear you. Every school wants a different essay. What a pain. Are you going to paint in here, too?"

I look around at the pastel-pink walls that seemed so sweet when I first moved in but don't match the new spread at all. "I'm thinking navy blue."

"Nice." Surface talk. Claire knows it, too. She stares at me, waiting.

I clear my throat. "I'll start, okay? About last night, like my grandmother always says, 'Never ruin a good apology with an excuse.'"

My friend bites her bottom lip and shakes her head. "You think there's an excuse for what you said to me, Sid?"

"No, that's exactly what I mean. There is none. Calling you selfish and saying that thing about the world revolving around you? It was wrong. Very wrong. I'm really sorry. And I don't really believe that. That's why I called you over here. To apologize."

Claire lets out a breath and leans back against my pillows, looking relieved. "It's fine. You were probably just upset about Trey." She shrugs. "And I shouldn't have accused you and Adam of being together behind my back, either."

"We would never do that!"

"I know. It's just that you both looked so guilty. And Adam was mad at me from the time I got to the party. It seems like you've been upset with me, too—or different, anyway—this whole summer."

"You think *I've* been different?"

I don't want to repeat our old argument from Nick's graduation party. So I begin to explain, or at least I try to, all the stuff that has been going on for me this summer. Like when she was depressed and avoiding me, how it felt like I'd lost my best friend. How even after we started hanging out together, it wasn't the same, because either Adam or Nellie were taking up all her time. And how last night, after I found out about Trey, and Adam said he'd been hurt by her, too, that something inside me just snapped.

"Claire? There is one more thing. I sort of told Adam what you said about not being ready to like anyone yet. Maybe that's another reason he was mad at you. Sorry."

"What?" She looks upset again, then she sighs. "I just knew you two were talking about me. But nothing else, right?"

"No. He gives really good hugs, though," I say, smiling.

"He's a touchy-feely kind of guy."

We both laugh. "But his hugs aren't as good as mine, right?" I say. She smiles when I put my arms around her, and she squeezes me even harder.

Then she hands me her phone with a picture of the two of them together. "He took me out for breakfast this morning. We're trying to work things out. He actually thinks I'm embarrassed of him. Can you believe it?"

I hesitate. "But you *do* act that way sometimes."

"Well, maybe," she admits. "But couldn't he have said that before? Like what if he's unhappy again? Is he just going to complain to all my friends behind my back?"

I pick up a garbage bag and tie it shut. "I hope not. But I won't talk to him about you anymore, okay? I promise."

"Thanks. That would be nice."

We watch some TV together until my grandmother comes home from work. After my room passes inspection, we decide to go for a drive. Grams has parked the van under a maple tree. It's only the first of September, but the leaves at the top of the tree are already beginning to turn red. With the sun less bright and a cool breeze blowing, I guess fall is almost here.

Claire points to the sidewalk where we immortalized our initials into the cement when the town was redoing the street, back in middle school: C.P. + S.M. in a heart, with B.F.F. underneath. Before boyfriends. Before everything.

Grams's van needs a wash. It's also got close to ninety-four thousand miles. After working all summer, I've saved some money. But the Eye-Scream store is closed for the season, and I still need to pay for insurance. Wonder if I'll ever get my own wheels.

Claire gets into the passenger side and puts on her seat belt. "You know, I don't miss driving at all."

Really? She was one of the first of us to get her license. I can understand how she must feel after everything, but she used to love cruising around. "You don't?"

"Well, maybe a little," she admits. "But hey, only nine months to go, and fifty hours of community service—till I get it back."

I do the quick math in my head. "Almost graduation."

Miles is shooting hoops in our driveway. Once our neighbor adjusted the basket, he started getting pretty good.

"Hey, guys, don't go yet," he calls. "I want to show you my jump shot, okay?"

"Do you mind?" I ask her. "Just for a few minutes?"

"Why not?" She lowers her window. "I'm so glad you're coming to the meet tomorrow, Sid. Wait till you see Tiny. What a trip! Did I tell you I've decided to compete again this year? My last year and then . . . I can't wait for college, can you?"

There she goes again, always looking at the future like it'll be better than the present—or the past. How can she be so sure?

"There's one thing I know I'm dreading. Trey will probably be home by then, too. But what if he brings that girl with him? She's from Massachusetts, did I tell you? What if I run into them together somewhere, like at the mall? Sometimes I think it might be easier if, you know—if he didn't come back at all."

"You don't really mean that!"

"No, I guess not."

She shakes her head. "This hasn't been easy for you, has it, Sid? I haven't been there for you this summer. Or all year. Not really. Not like a best friend should be. I'm sorry."

I smile. "It's okay. You're doing the best you can, right? I'm probably just mad at myself for wasting a whole year of my life, waiting for a stupid boy."

"But maybe it wasn't totally wasted. All that time you had for studying instead. You made honor roll, right?"

"*High* honors, baby!" We slap our palms together.

Miles makes a great shot from all the way over on the sidewalk. "Yay, Miles!" I say, so proud of him. "You're working so hard!"

Claire grins. "Oh, Sid. I almost forgot to tell you. My father said if you need a job this fall, he's got some openings at the store."

"But I thought he didn't trust any of your friends?"

"No, that's over. Besides, he always trusted you. And we had another talk when we got home last night. I guess my sister had told him what she remembered about the accident. I filled in the rest. So we're good now, I think. Dad even invited Adam to come out to dinner with our family next week."

"You mean *keg*-boy?"

"Seriously."

So, it looks like her family is all back together, happy-happy, again. The bummer is that it will probably never happen for me. And maybe that's why this break-up has hit me especially hard.

"You know what's really crazy, Claire? I honestly thought Trey and I would get married someday. I think it helped me not worry so much. Like about where Miles and I would end up if anything ever happened to my grandmother. You know Grams is getting old. She's not going to be around forever."

My friend looks over at my house, like somebody might overhear. "How can you say that? Pearl's not that old! She's got lots of good years ahead of her!"

"I know, but what if she doesn't? I'm not sure I can do *life* all by myself. I mean, who's going to walk me down the aisle someday? Not my dad, that's for sure. Did I tell you he's not coming up after all? Said his car won't make it. He told me maybe at Christmas—but I'm not holding my breath. And you know how my mom is. She definitely won't be able to pull together anything even resembling a bridal shower. All the things parents are supposed to do—who's going to be there for me?"

"I will." She acts like she really believes that.

"No, you won't. You'll go off somewhere, far away to college. I just know it. We'll grow apart. Don't even try to say we won't—because everyone I care about always leaves me—or something bad happens to them! So many things are going to be different after we graduate. I don't know. I just didn't think—"

She touches my hand to stop me. "Oh, Sid. We don't have to decide all that today, do we?"

"Maybe not. But sometimes life just seems so *unfair*, know what I mean?"

"You're right. It's not fair. What happened between you and Trey, what happened to Nellie? You can't expect life to always be fair, Sid."

"I know. But don't you ever wish things could have stayed the same? Like they were before the accident?"

We both look out the car window again. Some other little kids have joined Miles in a pickup game.

After a minute, Claire sighs. "I didn't appreciate how easy things were back then. If I've learned anything from all of this, it's that there's no going back. But change doesn't have to be bad. Maybe the trick is having faith that some good will come out of it. Somehow, it's got to, right?"

That sounds like something comforting Grams would say.

"Besides," Claire adds, "don't you know you're like a sister to me, Sid? My *other* sister? If we made it through all of this, almost all of high school, we're going to be friends forever. I just know it. And I'm not going to let you go through *forever* alone."

"You're not?"

"Not a chance." And this time I believe her.

"So, anyway," she says, "where should we all go for dinner next week? You're free on Friday night, right?"

"You mean you want me to come, too?"

She looks at me like I would be crazy to think anything else.

DON'T BE IMPATIENT. THERE IS PLENTY TO LEARN AND
PLENTY OF TIME IN WHICH TO LEARN IT.
—*Make the Team*

NELLIE'S BRAIN

At every gymnastics meet, the Judges sit on the same level as the Gymnasts, behind a table which is near either the apparatus they are judging or by the springy mats if they are judging the "floor." The standard rotation order is vault, bars, beam, and floor. All four events take place simultaneously, which for a Spectator can be quite stimulating. Where to focus? Not unlike a three-ring circus. *Vive* Cirque du Soleil!

Nellie is sitting barefoot on the mat, wearing her old team warm-up jacket and sweats. She is not competing, but when Claire asked permission from the Coach, Melissa said not only that she could but that Nellie *should* sit with the Team.

You would assume that our girl would be excited to be here. But the truth is, she is a bit overwhelmed by all the stimulation: the noise of Parents watching from the folding chairs; Spectators from the balcony above; the smell of popcorn and hamburgers from the foyer; and the feel of the mats, sticky with sweat beneath her.

Unfortunately, the doctors say that overstimulated is how she is going to be for up to a year—or more. Dr. Franks also said that Nellie must continue to go slowly in order to recover. Step by step. Small steps, like progressions in gymnastics. In these days of quick fixes and miraculous recoveries, it is not the best of news. *Alors*, but we all know that it could have been worse. Much worse.

As the famous poet Emily Dickinson once wrote, "All but Death can be adjusted."

I am not one to complain, but there *have* been moments in the past few months (just a few) when even I have felt like giving up, when the adjustments have seemed too hard to bear.

Yet, our girl's sunny disposition will not let me. She is a fighter, you see, a fierce competitor. Even after all that has happened, she is determined to keep on trying. Not that she is perfect by any means. We will continue to have our "bad" days, now and then.

But when she comes up feeling frustrated, I notice, is when she begins thinking about her Sister. Because Claire has had to take plenty of small steps, too. It helps that both girls have had good people standing beside them.

And that, *mes amis*, is exactly my point.

In the gymnasium, the Competitors fasten their tiger paws or wrist supports, and tape their knees or ankles, and stretch their limbs before the meet begins.

Three local club teams will be competing today. As they ease into their preperformance rituals, Nellie is scanning the group of Spectators for familiar faces. On the bleachers she sees that Sid has brought Miles along. He waves enthusiastically at Nellie.

Nellie waves back. "Hey, Sid! Hey, Miles!"

Our girl wants to tell Claire that Sid has arrived, but where did her Sister go? There are so many People here, so much to distract her. She looks at the front entrance of the gym. There is her Sister, standing by the door.

Oh, look! Nellie notices, *Adam is here, too!*

Nellie is happy that Adam decided to come today. Claire was worried that he was mad at her for judging him and they might break up. Nellie told her that she should just apologize already. Perhaps she took Nellie's advice?

As they greet each other, Nellie watches them kiss. She smiles. It is a kiss two People might give each other if they are beginning to fall in love. Nellie hopes to be kissed like that someday. Maybe in Paris?

Our girl still dreams of returning to Paris. She thinks it is the most romantic city.

Interrupting these thoughts, however, is the sudden appearance of a small, round-bellied Girl. "You're Nellie," she says, excited. "Right?"

"Hi?" Nellie replies, wondering if she has ever met this Girl before. Since the Accident, she's never quite sure whom she is supposed to know—or not.

"Hi," the Girl says. "I want to be just like you someday."

"You do?" Nellie asks, curious. "Why?"

"'Cause you're a champion. But first I have to not be scared of vault."

"Do I know you?" Nellie asks. The Girl's bright smile is contagious.

"No. They call me Tiny."

Now Nellie remembers something that Claire once told her. She is also thinking she might like this Tiny Girl.

It is time for the meet to begin. The Gymnasts parade out

in their sparkly uniforms, some with hearts or other symbols painted on their fresh faces. They present themselves to the Judges; it is tradition, raising their arms in the air. The crowd applauds. So much excitement in the building. Anything can happen.

As the meet progresses, Nellie watches Claire spot her Teammates, especially when they dismount from beam, but also on the uneven bars. They all seem to like her Sister, and that makes Nellie feel very proud.

The teammates begin to size up their competition. "The Yellow Jackets are our rivals," says Samantha. "Remember, Nellie?"

Yes, Nellie nods. She does remember this.

After each event, the Gymnast is awarded her score from the Judges on flip cards. The results are tallied, and then the entire Team moves together to the next apparatus. It is a close meet, and the time goes by quickly.

Nellie has decided to root for Tiny. The Girl did not do badly on the parallel bars. She only fell twice. Unfortunately her beam routine was a disaster. Her floor was only so-so. But now, getting ready to do her sprint for the vault, Tiny is hesitating. She is the last one to perform—in the last event of the day.

Nellie looks up at the score board. Their Team, Stand It Up, is trailing by a mere half point. At the far end of the gym, Claire stands, waiting to spot near the vault. She cups her hands. "You can do this, Tiny! Come on!"

The pressure is mounting. As Nellie watches, the tiny Girl gets halfway up the blue runway mat—but then she skitters off to the side. Nellie knows this is called a scratch, which means Tiny has only one more chance.

Tiny's Teammates on the mat nervously begin to whisper. Melissa and Claire also seem frustrated. Maybe Nellie can help?

She gets up and walks over to Tiny. The Girl looks like she wants to run out of the gym or disappear. "I can't do it!" she cries. "I'm going to let everyone down."

"Don't give up." Nellie takes the Girl's arm and straightens it, just a bit. "Try like this, 'K?"

"I *did* try it like that!" Tiny argues, shaking her head.

"No, you didn't." Nellie laughs. Claire was right; this one is stubborn.

"One more thing," Nellie adds. She bends down and whispers something into Tiny's ear.

"For real?" Tiny looks at her sideways but then nods. "Okay."

Tiny returns to the start of the runway. Hands on her hips, she looks determined. Nellie sits down next to the other Girls, who already seem resigned to losing. "Hey," she tells them. "Don't give up. Root for teammate."

"Okay. You can do it!" Samantha begins to yell, and the other girls do, too. "Show it off, Tiny! Push it, girl!"

Tiny begins to run, quickly increasing her speed. When she reaches the end of the mat, she jumps onto the springboard, puts her hands onto the vault, and kicks up her legs. Up and over she goes, to the soft foam mat on the other side.

Tiny takes only a small hop at the landing. Facing the Judges, she lifts her arms up in the air, then down. She actually remembers to smile.

Her score is a 6.3. It is enough.

Immediately, her Teammates explode up from the mat. They run over to the vault and surround her. "You did it! We won! We won!"

Claire rushes over, and Tiny leaps into her arms. Nellie watches them twirl around together and grins.

She remembers *exactly* how that feels. *Fantastique!*

⚬⚬

After the meet is over, the Girls gather in a small circle before they go up to receive their blue ribbons. Coach Melissa kneels by them, congratulating them, saying how well they did, how much they have improved, how much farther they all can go.

"You especially, Tiny. You did your best when it really mattered. We wouldn't have won today without you. Let's remember that this season, girls. Everybody counts."

Claire leans over to Nellie. "I worked with her the whole summer and still couldn't get her to do that. What's your secret? What did you say?"

Nellie whispers back, "Told her yell 'Kowabunga.'"

"What?" Claire laughs. She holds her stomach, because she cannot stop laughing. "That's it? Are you serious? That's all you said?"

"It used to help me." Nellie nods and pulls her knees into her chest. "When you get scared, got to think 'bout something else."

"Scared?" Claire shakes her head, incredulous. "You were the best, Nellie. Like *you* were ever scared."

Nellie shrugs. "Ever'body scared sometime, Claire."

"Maybe," she agrees with a catch in her voice. "But you're the bravest person I know."

Spectators and Girls are getting restless now, because it is almost time to go.

"Attention, everyone!" Melissa is talking into the microphone at the podium. "Could I have your attention, please?"

Melissa wants to thank the Parents and Guests for supporting them this afternoon. But before they go, she wants them to help her acknowledge an important member of their Team.

"This girl has worked very hard, overcoming extreme personal hardships this summer. She's been an inspiration to me, especially, but I think the team will agree, she's been an inspiration to all of us."

Nellie sees Claire gazing at her, but there is always room for one last surprise. Melissa claps her hands slowly. "Can we have a big round of applause for . . . *Claire* Perry?"

Everyone in the gym begins cheering. Nellie sees Adam and Sid and Miles jump up, whistling, with their hands above their heads.

How can there be so much joy on the heels of such sadness?

(I cannot pretend to know the answer, *mes amis*, there just is.)

And just when Nellie thinks her heart cannot hold any more happiness, the Coach asks Claire if there is anything she would like to say.

Claire comes up to the podium. "Thanks, Melissa. Actually, I think my *sister's* the one who's worked hard this summer. She's come a very long way. And she's going to keep working. She wants to try to compete again, right, Nellie?"

Nellie smiles and gives her a thumbs-up sign.

"But mostly, Nellie told me, she wants to have fun. And whenever she's ready to compete again—and I'm not saying *if,* but *when*—I'll be there to support her. Because if anyone can do this," Claire adds, "I know you can, Nellie. You're *my* hero. You were totally meant to fly."

Melissa motions for Nellie to join them at the podium. Nellie gets up and begins to step carefully across the mat— but, unfortunately, not carefully enough. Her toe misses an edge—and she trips and almost falls!

Claire rushes over to steady her. "Don't worry. I've got you."

"Always do," Nellie replies, beaming.

Claire pauses. "Well, maybe there were a few times before when I didn't. But not anymore. I'll be here to spot you forever. I promise."

Nellie leans forward and says something to Claire. It is loud in the gym, so Nellie decides to say it again.

You might be wondering what it was, since Claire has begun to cry.

"Not just for me," Nellie repeats slowly, one word at a time. "For each other, 'K?"

Traumatic brain injury (TBI) is a leading cause of death and lifelong disability among children and young adults in the United States. The Centers for Disease Control and Prevention (CDC) has estimated that each year, around 1.5 million Americans survive a TBI, 230,000 of whom are hospitalized. Approximately 50,000 Americans die each year following a TBI, representing one-third of all injury-related deaths. Adolescents, young adults, and the elderly are at greatest risk of these injuries. Brain injuries, from mild to severe, account for an estimated 22 percent of all troops' injuries in Afghanistan and Iraq. About half of all TBIs are caused by motor vehicle accidents, almost half of which involve the use of alcohol.

Acknowledgments

I started writing this novel in early 2005, after a boy driving at high speed crashed his car less than one mile from our home. Fortunately both he and his passenger walked away from that accident—but it got me thinking: what if they hadn't?

Tragically, in the time it has taken to complete this book, four teens (in less than three years) from our local high school have died in driving (or boating) and alcohol-related incidents—too much for one community to bear. My heart goes out to anyone who has been affected by the untimely death or serious injury of a young person and to those who are working so hard at prevention.

Many people helped in the writing process. My everlasting thanks to: **Don Judson**, the best book coach *ever*; **Melissa Gendreau** (Mt. Hope High Gymnastics Coach) for insights into girls' gymnastics; **Cindy Butts,** on being the parent of a gymnast; **Nancy Skilton** for French translation assistance; **Jill Banister**, R.N., for feeding tube and other medical information; my tumbling niece, **Carly**, for "follow your fingers"; **Penny Morris** for getting me to the real quahoggers; **Michalea Morris** for "pinhead on a swan neck"; **Kathy Sullivan** and **Joanne Royley** and **Barrington's Substance Abuse Task Force**—where I am a proud, although not always active, member; **Gabrielle Abbate** (Executive Director of M.A.D.D., R.I. Chapter); and **Chief John LaCross** (Barrington, R.I., Police Department) and **Detective Joe Amorosa** (Providence, R.I., Police Department) for information about the consequences of driving recklessly or impaired; **Tracy Schott** (Max Films) for suggestions on cover art; **Arlene Lischko** and **Claudia Gordon,** best first readers; **Brooke,** my favorite fan.

And a special, heartfelt thanks to **Marilyn Brigham,** my wonderful editor, for her refusal to give up on this book until it reached its very best; **Margery Cuyler;** and the rest of the fabulous team at Marshall Cavendish; also **Susan Schulman,** my agent, who offered expert guidance.

A special thank you to all of the young people who have shared their stories with me in my therapy office; I hope I have listened well. And finally to my husband, Mark, and our two sons, for their love and sustenance beyond measure.

The following were helpful in researching for this novel:

Web sites

The Brain Injury Association of America: www.biausa.org
USA Gymnastics: www.usa-gymnastics.org
About Gymnastics: www.gymnastics.about.com

Books

Carpenter, Linda Jean. *Gymnastics for Girls and Women*. West Nyack, NY: Parker Pub. Co., 1984.

Johansen, Ruthann Knechel. *Listening in the Silence, Seeing in the Dark: Reconstructing Life after Brain Injury*. Berkeley: University of California Press, 2002.

Osborn, Claudia L. *Over My Head: A Doctor's Story of Head Injury from the Inside Looking Out*. Kansas City, MO: Andrews McMeel Publishing, LLC, 1998.

Schoenbrodt, Lisa, ed. *Children with Traumatic Brain Injury: A Parent's Guide*. Bethesda, MD: Woodbine House, 2001.

Sey, Jennifer. *Chalked Up: Inside Elite Gymnastics' Merciless Coaching, Overzealous Parents, Eating Disorders, and Elusive Olympic Dreams*. New York: William Morrow, 2008.

Whitlock, Steve, for The U.S. Gymnastics Federation. *Make the Team: Gymnastics for Girls: A Gold Medal Guide for Great Gymnastics*. Boston: Little, Brown, 1991.

DVDs
The HBO family and R.A.D.D. *Smashed: Toxic Tales of Teens and Alcohol*. Home Box Office Inc., 2004.